PRAISE FOR MAKING

"Although other books and literature have identified the problems with making positive change, *Making Feedback Work* provides a clear, concise, and immediately useable plan of action. Folkman makes no false promises about the ease of effective change but accurately describes the formula for success. It's realistic."

—Bob Osswald, Vice President of Development and Training,
AutoZone

"A great resource for the practical end of the survey process, including many useful stories and examples, *Making Feedback Work* boils down the concepts and theories into useful principles."

—Kirby Yoder, OE Consultant,
Eli Lilly and Company

"I really appreciated Folkman's insights into why and how people change from feedback. Joe's information really hit the nail on the head."

—Susan Edlinger, Manager of Employee Development,
Litton Industries

"*Making Feedback Work* addresses one of the most critical factors for ensuring that employee surveys are a success in the organization. Folkman provides practical strategies and tools to help organizations do something about the feedback received from employee 'climate' surveys. The principles will help organizations better manage the 'people' part of their business."

—Vince Butterfield, Organizational Consultant,
Weyerhaeuser

"Joe Folkman provides a very useful guide for individuals and organizations interested in improving performance, with great stories, insights, and experiences that support key principles to change."

—Mario Gosalvez, Performance Technologist,
Hewlett-Packard

"Folkman's exceptional summary makes it crystal clear that surveying employees is not just an interesting activity: Value creation comes from using survey data to develop and implement specific action plans. Those seeking to drive their organizations to exceptional performance will appreciate Joe's road-map!"

—Steve Raschilla, Consultant, World Business Group,
Amoco

"Organizational feedback is a labyrinth through which many wander. Joe Folkman guides us through this complex field with clear principles, practical insights, and real-world examples. The alternative is to get lost in the maze."

—Ron Burbridge, Vice President of HR Effectiveness,
Canadian Imperial Bank of Commerce

MAKING

FEEDBACK

WORK

Turning Feedback from Employee
Surveys into Change

Joe Folkman, Ph.D.

The publisher offers discounts on this book when ordered in bulk quantities. To place your order, or to get more information about Novations, Joe Folkman, or the survey instruments described in this book, please contact Novations Group, Inc., at:

Novations Group, Inc.
5314 North 250 West, Suite 320
Provo, UT 84604
phone: (801) 375-7525
fax: (801) 375-7595
www.novations.com

Note: Some of the material in this work has been adapted from Joe Folkman, *Turning Feedback into Change,* Provo, UT: Novations Group, Inc., © 1996 Joseph R. Folkman.

Editorial/Design/Production:

Executive Excellence Publishing
1344 East 1120 South
Provo, UT 84604
phone: (801) 375-4060
fax: (801) 377-5960
www.eep.com

DEDICATION

Over 20 years ago two of my professors, Gene Dalton and Bill Dyer, asked me to work with them on marketing and supporting their Organizational Analysis Survey. Gene and Bill had designed the survey as a way to measure issues that were critical to organizational success. They had no background in psychometrics; they were change agents and were more interested in creating a platform for change than in making statistical comparisons and algorithms. What I learned from Gene and Bill was that, ultimately, the change is what organizations want—not the data. In 1997, both Gene and Bill passed away. Part of the legacy they left was their focus on change and their desire to teach people how to facilitate the change process in organizations.

TABLE OF CONTENTS

1

INTRODUCTION

Most organizations don't lack feedback on how they could improve their performance, communication, or teamwork. For many companies, the typical reaction to new feedback is, "So what, we're too busy to do anything about it anyway."

To the question, "In the last month has your organization received any feedback or suggestions on how things might be improved?" the majority of managers would answer, "Yes." But to the follow-up question, "Has your company made any improvements or changes because of that feedback?" the likely reply would be, "No." Likewise, if you ask managers, "Do you know of any ideas that, if implemented, would make your organization more effective?" most of them would reply, "Yes." But most feel they can only juggle so many balls, and many of those ideas remain unimplemented.

Most organizations receive much more feedback than they are willing or able to implement. They receive feedback from many sources, including books, articles, speeches, competitors, customers, and employees. To cope with all this information, some stop listening; others become defensive. Some blame others, and others simply ignore the feedback. This reminds me of a Vermont farmer joke: An agricultural agent goes to visit a local farmer. After observing the operation, the agent asks the farmer if he would like some suggestions on how the farm could be improved. The farmer replies, "No," to which the agent asks, "Why not?" The farmer answers, "I already know at least fifty things I ought to be doing to run this farm better, and I don't do any of them. Why should I add more to the list?"

The growing trend in business seems to be to provide individuals and teams with more and more feedback on their performance strengths and weaknesses. Companies have instituted business reviews, customer surveys, employee surveys, and regular performance reviews. They have tried upward evaluations, 360-degree or four-way feedback evaluations, and peer evaluations. Most of these companies are implementing new information systems to make almost instantaneous changes in budgets, production, sales, and employee data. The idea behind the trend is that the more information and feedback people in the organization receive, and the more authority or empowerment they have to make decisions on that information, the more effective they will be.

And, to no one's surprise, obtaining feedback from employees has been determined to be an effective way for organizations to discover their strengths and weaknesses. Feedback from employees frequently helps organizations understand aspects of the company that would not otherwise be apparent to top leaders, but which are obvious to others.

But, although managers are receiving more feedback, a reciprocal amount of change does not seem to be taking place, at least not from employee perspectives. In fact, just like antibiotics that are used too frequently, managers in organizations start to build immunities to feedback and to forcefully resist new changes.

Our research at Novations Group has uncovered several clear and defined principles of feedback that generally seem to apply in most interactions involving feedback. The first is:

Principle 1: Asking others for input increases their expectation that you will change in a positive way.

Many who receive feedback turn that feedback into measurable change. However, others receiving feedback do not change. This frustrates not only those who receive the feedback, but also those who provide the feedback. This leads to the second principle:

Principle 2: If you receive feedback but do not change for the better, you will be perceived more negatively than if you had not received feedback.

The purpose of this book is to help you and your organization accept, prioritize, plan for, and change as a result of the feedback you receive from employees. The approach I use has been refined through experience in working with thousands of people in organizations who have received feedback. Those who use feedback to create organizational change are not necessarily stronger or smarter than those who don't, but they follow a few simple principles and steps that make lasting and positive changes possible.

2

REACTING TO FEEDBACK

When people receive feedback, they typically react. These reactions range from extremely negative to extremely positive, or there may be no visible reaction at all.

Principle 3: You cannot change what you do not believe needs to be changed.

The feedback experience is fundamentally different from looking at production reports or accounting statements. Even though someone may provide feedback in a way that would leave no doubt or difficulty in understanding, this does not necessarily guarantee that people will believe the feedback and act on it. Those who receive feedback and then make changes or adjustments in their organizations experience greater effectiveness because of that feedback.

Principle 4: It is better to receive negative feedback than to receive no feedback at all.

Situations in which no feedback is given can be frustrating. Imagine how you would feel if you had just finished putting a lot of effort into studying a subject, taking a test, and then never knowing how well you performed on the test. You would never be able to improve, right? We should perceive feedback as a welcome opportunity, not a dreaded obligation. Having an appropriate attitude toward feedback can be extremely beneficial, and the process of making feedback work starts with accepting the feedback given.

Denial

One skill that each of us has developed to protect our fragile egos is denial. When we were children and our friends or siblings teased us, we developed the ability to say, "You're wrong! I'm not like that!" Now that we have grown up, we often demonstrate that ability whenever we receive negative feedback.

Principle 5: Rather than accept insults and abuse, we tend to denounce not only what is said but those who say it.

Most of us move from childhood to adulthood through a maturation process that makes us more effective as adults than as children. However, because children have not had the years of practice in rejecting negative feedback, most of them are substantially more effective at accepting feedback than adults. The extent to which you have developed your denial skills determines the extent to which you accept feedback or question its accuracy.

Levels of Denial

When you receive feedback from others, if you're like most people, you pass through some level of denial. If you feel your feedback does not point out any specific areas of change for the organization, you may be right—or you may be denying or ignoring some data. Likewise, if you think the feedback does not accurately reflect the true performance of the organization, you may be right—or the feedback may be so threatening that you simply rationalize it away.

Minimal denial presents itself as rationalization. At this level, when people receive negative feedback, they rationalize that it isn't important to change, or perhaps they feel things "aren't so bad." People who exercise minimal denial are generally more aware of their rationalizations and often can be persuaded to accept the feedback.

Moderate denial is less conscious. In this situation, people react to feedback, but they usually do not know why they are reacting. Typically, people with moderate denial display either more emotion or almost no emotion. Some people in moderate denial confront others, blaming them for the negative feedback. Others have no emotional reaction to feedback and try to minimize its importance.

Those who experience *advanced denial* are not conscious that they are in denial. They may act as experts and assertively deny that a problem exists, or they may totally ignore the feedback. The difference is they are not consciously aware of what they are doing.

Perceptions Are Reality

A key to understanding feedback is to work through your denial and believe that the perceptions of others are, in fact, reality. Our experience suggests that the most productive approach to handling data is this:

Principle 6: You can safely assume that all perceptions are real, at least to those who own them.

> *After reviewing his feedback on how well he gives effective instructions, and discovering the very low ratings given him by his direct reports, Steve commented, "They're wrong; I give great instructions. Those guys are just too dense to understand. The problem is not with my instructions; it's with the audience I give them to."*

Steve believed his perceptions were real and that his direct reports' perceptions were wrong. Steve may be effective at giving instructions to highly trained personnel, but if his job requires that his direct reports understand his instructions, and if his instructions confuse the direct reports, then he is not effective.

Even when perceptions are completely inaccurate, they still represent reality. A mechanical engineer once illustrated this point:

> *Suppose I were to build a structurally sound and safe bridge that adheres to all laws and principles of engineering. But, because of the unique design of the bridge, most people perceive my bridge is not safe or structurally sound.*
>
> *It is clear to me that those perceptions may not be true, but to the people who believe the bridge is unsafe, the perceptions are real. If the bridge were built to help people cross a river, but people think the bridge is unsafe and therefore do not use the bridge, of what value would my bridge be?*

Balance

When receiving feedback, some reactive behaviors are counterproductive. However, productive behaviors are not always the simple opposites of counterproductive behaviors. For example, one counterproductive behavior is rationalization. When people rationalize away the results of feedback surveys, they convince themselves nothing is wrong. They discount the feedback or even reject it outright. Such actions are counterproductive. However, we also find that the opposite of such behavior, often perceived as more productive— such as taking the results of a survey too literally—is also counterproductive. For example, others may try to encourage them simply to accept the feedback at face value without trying to find reasons why the feedback could be wrong, or they read more into the feedback than was originally intended.

Principle 7: You need to balance the interpretation of survey feedback to deal effectively with it.

Balance is the key to effectively dealing with feedback. For example, you must be able to balance between rationalization and literal interpretation of data. Effectively dealing with survey data may require some rationalization, but it may also require some taking of results at face value.

Those who deal most effectively with feedback are those who maintain a balance between these two counterproductive behaviors. For most people, such balance is difficult to achieve. Most people want to be told to do one thing and not to do another, but balance requires that we do a little of one and a little of the other, and not carry any one behavior to an extreme.

The following are four extremes, or common coping strategies, that require balance:

1. Rationalization versus Literal Acceptance
2. Fight versus Flight
3. "That's Interesting" versus "That's Terrible"
4. Paralysis of Analysis versus "Why Bother?"

Rationalization Versus Literal Acceptance

When people rationalize away the results of their feedback, they often are trying to justify their own behavior while avoiding the underlying sources of the problem. Here is an example:

> *While reviewing her survey feedback, Jill found that the data described her work unit as bureaucratic. When asked about the results, Jill said, "I know most of my direct reports feel there is too much red tape and bureaucracy in our work unit, but*

*they're wrong. We have procedures given to us from
upper management, and we simply have to follow
them. I didn't make up most of the procedures, but
it's my job to be sure the people in my group follow
the procedures and conform to the rules. If people
would just accept the rules and policies and quit
complaining, there would be no problem."*

Jill rationalized away the feedback from her group, blaming the problem on upper management. Some people have great rationalizing skills. The process typically involves making excuses, justifying behavior, or discrediting feedback.

Rationalization is counterproductive. We often respond to rationalization by encouraging people to accept their feedback at face value. However, some managers avoid having to think too deeply by accepting the results of their feedback surveys too literally. Here is one example:

*As he reviewed the feedback from the employee
survey, John became confused. The overall results
from his division showed an average score for candor.
However, when the data was broken out by position,
it indicated that managers at his level and above
rated candor very high while hourly employees rated
it fairly low. He showed the results to the human
resources manager and asked, "Who's right?"*

She replied, "Both groups are right."

*Her response frustrated John. He responded, "Either
we have candor in this organization or we don't."*

People don't always agree on the meaning of survey results because individuals respond differently to the same experiences. For example, in John's case he felt that candor meant having an open door. He would often say, "Anyone can come and talk to me about anything they want, and I will listen." This was, in fact, true. Most managers who regularly interacted with John knew that if they had something to discuss, John would be open to listen. They found that he liked to "push" for answers to unresolved issues, trying to bring out the best in other managers.

But the experience was not always easy for direct reports and other employees. Whenever difficult issues came up, John had the ability to intimidate with his disarming questions. He liked to test people's convictions. Managers who were self-confident knew what John was doing and did not mind engaging him in a debate. On the other hand, although those who reported to John knew his door was always open, they rarely were invited to discuss anything. Further, whenever direct reports tried to discuss issues that applied to them, John would go into his assertive questioning mode. The direct reports would interpret this as defensive behavior and would never try to engage in a debate with him. So, because of the mutually supportive relationships he had with managers, John and the other managers saw a culture of candor, but, at the same time, the hourly employees only saw mistrust and frustration.

Fight Versus Flight

Another common strategy for avoiding having to deal with unexpected feedback is to "fight." Here is one example:

> *As the divisional director of a high-tech manufacturing company reviewed the results of a survey given to all division employees, it became evident that, for the most part, the results were not positive. The director's frustration and anger began to grow, but he did a good job of keeping it to himself.*
>
> *Later, when the consultants who administered the survey presented the results on an overhead projector, additional negative results were indicated. Also, the director noticed a typo on the overhead slide. The*

director pounded on the table and said in a loud voice, "There's a typo on that page! Does this represent the quality of your work? How do I know there aren't more errors throughout the rest of the data? I refuse to listen to anything else until you people get your act together." With that, he left the room.

In the foregoing example, I was a graduate student at the time, assisting the consultants to make the presentation. As the director walked out of the room, I felt speechless. I remember thinking to myself, "We blew it; we made a typo. We are responsible for the fact that he didn't receive the feedback."

A few minutes later, the team that had presented the results started to discuss what had happened. Someone asked, "Does he always react that way to typos?" An internal consultant responded, "Only when he doesn't like what he's hearing."

The director's reaction to the survey data was to fight. His rejection of the survey results prevented the organization from having to change, but it also kept it from improving. The issues presented didn't go away just because he refused to listen to them. This case is similar to a case study used in many introductory psychology classes. The study describes a patient in a mental institution who believes he is dead. The therapist assigned to the patient spends one hour, every day, talking about what dead people do that is different from people who are alive.

The therapist asks, "Can dead people talk?"

"Yes, dead people can talk," replied the patient.

The therapist continues to review every behavior, thought process, and physical condition, until finally, after weeks of therapy, he asks the patient, "Do dead people bleed?"

"No," replied the patient, "dead people don't bleed."

The therapist feels ecstatic. He is sure he has found the cure. Quickly he runs to find a small pin. He grabs the patient's hand, pricks it with the pin, and watches the patient's reaction. As the patient watches the blood ooze from his finger he appears astonished. Looking up at the therapist, he exclaims, "Gee, I guess I was wrong. Dead people *do* bleed."

Although fighting the data or trying to prove it wrong may be counterproductive, the other extreme, "flight," is also counterproductive. People who engage in flight, or escape, behavior often believe all the survey results without question, typically focusing only on the negative aspects. One manager reviewed her results and commented, "I always knew I was bad; this data simply confirms it." While people in fight mode disagree with their survey results, those in flight mode often try to hide from, ignore, or allow themselves to be destroyed by the results. This tactic allows the feedback recipient to avoid the problem by escaping from it.

Why is the process of receiving feedback so threatening? Most people spend an exorbitant amount of time and energy trying to hide any evidence of incompetence. This is one of the reasons we go to school, get degrees, become supervisors, seek impressive job titles, and hang plaques on the wall. However, we all retain some level of incompetence in many life areas. Most of us have a few fears tucked away in the back of our minds about what would happen if others knew we were not competent.

> *Ellen's mood changed from enthusiastic and bubbly to gloomy when she received her feedback. Each page of the survey felt like a knife being stabbed into her back. As Ellen read through the written comments, she shook her head in disbelief.*
>
> *As the day ended, the facilitator pulled Ellen aside and asked her to stay and talk for a few minutes. As soon as everyone had left, the facilitator asked, "So Ellen, how is it going?"*
>
> *That was all it took to release the torrents of tears Ellen had been saving up for almost three*

hours. She showed her report to the facilitator. Although she found herself above the norm in most areas, she had been below the norm in several others. Written comments pointed out weaknesses such as, "Ellen never really lets me know where I stand. She always tells me I'm doing fine, but I don't really believe her because she tells everybody that."

Ellen described herself as a very positive person. She thought that since taking over the group she had won over most of the employees in the group and that they had become her friends. But, she wondered, "How could they do this to me? How could they say such negative things if they were friends?"

Ellen's data actually had been much more positive than several others in the class, and nothing in her survey's written comments had been extremely negative.

The next day several other participants shared their results with her. After seeing how negative people could be, Ellen came to realize that the results of her survey actually had been quite good. At that point, she began to acknowledge some of the criticism without feeling she had been stabbed in the back.

"That's Interesting" Versus "That's Terrible"

Although some people believe receiving bad survey data means the end of the world, other people read their results as if they were unrelated technical reports. A major factor associated with creating change is this law:

Principle 8: People must have a "felt need" to change, or they will not change.

Because our business environments encourage a bias toward rational, unemotional, or logical thinking, many people develop a "that's interesting" view toward their feedback.

One engineering manager who had received extremely negative data remarked, "These are very interesting results, and I'm going to study them until I understand them fully."

Cigarette smoking is a useful analogy. Most people who smoke understand that smoking is hazardous to their health. Many smokers know they ought to quit. But even though people know smoking is not good for them, and they would like to quit, many never quit because they do not have a large enough "felt need." One man, after attempting to quit smoking several times, finally succeeded. He said, "I was able to quit when I wanted to quit more than I wanted to smoke." In other words, he was able to quit when he had a large enough "felt need" to change.

The other side of "that's interesting" is similar to the "flight" mentality. In the "that's terrible" state, people react as if shattered by each piece of negative feedback. People who don't have enough felt need to change, but who continue to get negative feedback, often talk about getting another position or moving to another company. They will do anything other than discuss the results and consider appropriate changes.

Paralysis of Analysis Versus "Why Bother?"

In some cases, those who prefer not to avoid the results of their feedback go too far, and they end up applying a totally different avoidance strategy: the paralysis of analysis. They become so overwhelmed by what appears necessary for improvement that they avoid action. Here is an example:

> *Kathy, an accountant, began to analyze the employee survey results for her group. The first report she received provided the aggregate results for her department. After reviewing the results of the department, Kathy asked to see the results of her group broken out by position. Then, noting that she had enough people in the professional and salaried-exempt categories, she asked for two additional*

*breakouts. These reports helped her determine if neg-
ative issues were present in the results for each group.*

*A few days later, Kathy requested additional
breakouts for her group by gender, age, and location.
Employees in her group began to get nervous about all
the analysis. They wondered if Kathy was looking
for issues or trying to isolate who said what. When
asked what additional insights she hoped to find in
the additional analysis, she responded, "I might find
out something new." But, when asked if the data she
had already seen had clearly identified several issues
that needed change, she indicated that they did.*

Soon after this, Kathy realized that asking for more analysis had been a convenient way to avoid the issues identified
by the survey. Those issues were personally threatening to
her, and she had hoped to find groups, such as women or
men, or older or younger employees, who differed in their
opinion from the overall results.

The following contrasting example shows how others
sometimes see no need to explore their own feedback at all:

*Rand heard the assignment clearly: "Find at
least three areas that need improvement and list
them in the action planning booklet." Rand breezed
through his numeric data and written comments
and found what he was looking for: the 15 most
negative items. He quickly read the first three
items, transferred them word for word into his booklet, and then closed the booklet. He passed the booklet to the manager and said, "I've completed the
assignment; what now?"*

Rand also might have considered the following questions:
"Am I sure these are the most negative issues?" "How do
these issues correlate with the written comments?" "Will

changes in these areas have the greatest impact on the performance of our work group?" "Perhaps I ought to consider working on the fourth most negative item; it reads: 'Fails to make decisions based on the best available data.' "

When you receive feedback, you must be willing to dig in and find the facts while not getting yourself bogged down in the analysis.

Attitudes About Feedback

If perceptions are reality and striking an appropriate balance is important, what is the most effective way to process feedback? One way is to consider your attitude toward receiving feedback. The following attitudes are helpful:

- *I enjoy feedback; I would rather receive negative feedback than no feedback at all.* We should constantly look for ways to receive feedback because it's a learning opportunity.
- *I know feedback is difficult to give and often uncomfortable for others to provide.* Attacking those who provide feedback is an excellent way to prevent yourself from getting more. Instead of attacking, let others know their input is appreciated. Appreciate the fact that someone has taken the effort, time, and personal risk to provide you with feedback, even if you don't agree with it.
- *I know feedback can be both positive and negative, and I first look at the positive to reinforce the things I do well.* Try to avoid looking for the negative and expecting the worst.
- *I believe I can facilitate change and improvement in my organization.* Employees expect something to be done about their feedback. Commit to finding something you can do something about. Make some changes. Report to those providing feedback about the things you choose not to change and how you plan to improve in the areas you are willing to change.

3

WHY DID I GET THAT FEEDBACK?

The process of forming impressions and making attributions about others and about events has been extensively researched. This chapter explores how others form impressions of us, or about events, and how those impressions differ from our own.

Principle 9: Others see things differently than we see them.

My history professor used to say that those who don't understand history are doomed to repeat it. I feel the same way about how people form impressions and make attributions about behavior. Understanding the process helps us answer the question, "Why do others perceive things differently than I perceive them?" Understanding how impression formation and attribution work helps us make the process work for us instead of against us.

The perceptions others have are real. People can't be talked out of their impressions. Those impressions are created from what they observe and experience, and, to change those impressions, we must first understand how people see and experience events.

Principle 10: To change the impressions others have, we must first understand how they see and experience things.

Sometimes, the impressions others have are not accurate from our point of view. Understanding the attribution process helps us and others form a more accurate perception of reality.

Forming Impressions

It's amazing how quickly we form impressions. Based on very limited information, we might conclude, "This work group is very productive and efficient," or "This work group is unproductive and inefficient."

How do you form impressions of events? Do you use a rational approach, considering every observation as if solving a math problem, or do you take all the things you observe and add them up to form an overall impression? Solomon Asch researched this question and examined two possible techniques. One technique is to consider traits individually and then formulate an overall impression. The following example demonstrates this additive approach:

Overall Impression = Trait A + Trait B + Trait C + Trait D

The second technique is to consider the interaction of all elements to form an overall impression. To demonstrate this, place drops of several different colors of food coloring into water. We do not see the individual colors for very long because they blend with the other colors. The overall impression we receive is the result of the overall color we see.[1] Our overall impression tends to bias our focus on individual elements. If our overall impression is positive, then we tend to overlook some faults. On the other hand, if our overall impression is negative, many positive things are overlooked. *(See Figure 1.)*

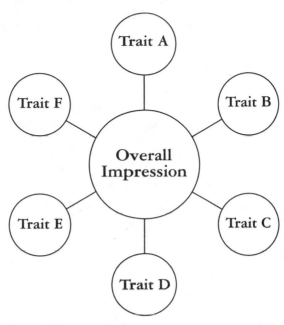

Figure 1: Overall Impression

Asch found that, rather than looking at individual elements, we see the interaction of those elements and form an
overall impression. We see things as a total package, rather
than as a sum of small elements.

> *Charlie had recently taken over a group of bus
> drivers who were subcontracted to transport company
> employees from town to the work site. The contract
> between the bus drivers and the company had been
> renegotiated just a few weeks before Charlie was
> given his new assignment. Under the old contract,
> drivers were compensated for eight hours of work
> each day regardless of how much time they spent
> driving the bus. During that period, most of the
> drivers would pick up the employees in the morning,
> take them to the work site, and then hang out in the
> lounge for six or seven hours before taking the
> employees home. But, under the new contract, drivers*

had to work during the time they were at the site in order to be paid. If they sat in the lounge, they would be paid only for four hours of work.

An employee survey was conducted shortly after Charlie took over the group. The results from the survey were extremely negative, and Charlie was very disappointed. He had worked hard to create a positive work environment for the drivers. He had sat down with each driver to explore work options for the time at the site. But, after looking at the data he concluded, "I guess I didn't do any good at all. Why don't these employees see the good things I do?"

Charlie's experience closely follows what Solomon Asch found: People don't objectively judge individual issues; they bundle them collectively. We tend to rationalize individual characteristics to conform with an overall judgment. Charlie's employees, like most people, would have a difficult time reconciling an overall negative impression with outstanding performance in certain areas. Instead, they attributed lower performance in all areas to make sense of their overall impressions.

Inconsistencies in performance (such as doing well at some things but poorly at others) cause us to search for sensible ways to rationalize those inconsistencies. So, either we change our overall impression, or we ignore performance in some areas to maintain our overall impression. It is generally easier to ignore a few things that do not fit with our impression than to change our overall impression.

Asch also found that some traits have greater influence on the overall impression than others. Sometimes we may acknowledge weaknesses in a key area but rationalize them because of strengths in other areas. However, if those weaknesses are in critical areas, they may have a substantial influence on our overall impression.

Packaging

As we observe the behavior and performance of others, we tend to "package" the information we receive. Think of the process as similar to having some large bundles of traits, attributes, and behaviors. After observing someone for a period of time, we form an overall impression of them.

Most people have a "library" of favorite words they use to describe different people or groups. After some observation, we select one stereotype and assign it to a person or group. Many of the traits, attributes, and behaviors fit the type, but others do not. But, because we tend to hold the bundle together, we don't closely scrutinize the attributes that don't fit. For example, suppose you knew a work group that was very technically competent. You might also assume that the group is analytical in its decision making. Many technically competent groups are not analytical, but, because you have bundled "technically competent" and "analytical," you assume that technically competent people are analytical. Such packaging can bias our impressions either positively or negatively.

In your feedback, you may find that, as a result of packaging, others attribute positive or negative traits to you or your group which you don't actually have.

> *After a series of focus group interviews, it was clear that employees were frustrated with the human resources department. It also was evident that the department was perceived as inconsistent and unfair in how it applied company policies. Hourly employees had a particularly negative view of the department.*
>
> *After hearing the feedback, the human resources manager reacted, "The reality is that HR is very consistent and fair. All we are doing is enforcing the official policies of this organization. We don't hear about all incidents, but when we do our policies are clear, and we feel it is our responsibility to act*

according to company policies. If someone shows up to work and has been drinking, the policy is clear about the disciplinary action that should be taken. Many managers throughout the plant may ignore flagrant violations of company policies, and the hourly employees may see some people getting away with things, but, when we get involved, we stick to the policies. So, because of this, we are the bad guys; every manager likes to put the blame on us."

In this example, it did not appear the human resources manager was avoiding the feedback. Instead, the feedback seemed to reflect the hourly employees' perspectives about company discipline in general. So, because the managers tended to overlook occasional violations and the human resources department often acted quickly and decisively whenever it became aware of violations, the hourly employees perceived the whole company as inconsistent and unfair. They "packaged" their overall perception about company discipline in their responses to the human resources survey, even though the human resources department was not entirely responsible for that perception.

The Halo Effect

The "halo effect" refers to the way our perceptions may be altered, either positively or negatively, because of an overall impression. For example, we tend to perceive other people as physically attractive if we like them.

Charles Dailey found that once people form an impression based on limited data, they are not as open to information which contradicts the original impression. Our perceptions are also heavily influenced by position, status, roles, and responsibilities. We have expectations about how people or groups ought to perform, and we tend to judge them based on those expectations, frequently ignoring the specifics of the situation.[2]

The idea of the halo effect came about from research into employee morale. Researchers measured employee morale and then made changes to the work environment that shouldn't have had anything to do with morale, such as changing the amount of light in the work area. They then measured morale again, and it had improved. What did changing the lights have to do with morale? Nothing directly, but employees saw special attention being paid to their group and reacted positively.

Explaining Others' Behavior

Principle 11: When we provide feedback, we tend to base our perceptions on our own performance and personality.

Alvin Scodel and Paul Mussen found that people who were considered highly authoritarian rated low authoritarians about as authoritarian as themselves. On the other hand, people who were considered low in authoritarianism rated high authoritarians as much more authoritarian than themselves. Research on dogmatism, sociability, and liberal-conservative ratings also confirm that the characteristics of the raters have a significant effect on the rating.[3] This should not come as a big surprise. Most of us are aware that managers, hourly employees, and various other professionals such as engineers, accountants, attorneys, programmers, researchers, or educators, tend to like people who act and think the same way they do.

Suppose you saw a person kicking a dog. If you were asked to explain why the person kicked the dog, your explanation would typically involve one of two different approaches. One approach would be to interpret the person's attitude toward the dog: "This person is mean and hates dogs." Another approach would be to interpret the person's environment or situation as a possible motivation: "The dog tried to bite him."

Harold Kelley describes four techniques people use to judge whether actions should be attributed to a person or group's attitude, or to the environment or situation:

Is the action distinctive? Does this action occur separate from other actions? Is it unique? If we don't see the person's actions as distinctive, we tend not to attribute the person's action to a unique situation.

Is the action consistent over time? Any person or group can achieve top performance or fail once or twice. One explanation for such performance could be situational, or "luck." On the other hand, if the same performance occurs consistently, we tend to see it as an attribute of the person or group.

Is the action consistent over situations? Can this person or group maintain this same action in a variety of situations? If a person or group performs well in one assignment but fails in another, the failure in the second tends to cancel out any success in the first, however significant.

Is there consensus? Is the action of the person or group similar to others who are known to have these qualities? Do others I know agree with me on the action? We tend to make comparisons before we make judgments.[4]

As we judge the performance of a person or group, we generally use criteria similar to these to determine whether what the group or person does is a function of skill (or lack of skill), or the situation.

One fascinating aspect of attribution is that people and groups typically attribute their own failure to factors in the environment. For example: "We failed because they made that job too difficult," or "We failed because we had bad luck." On the other hand, we tend to attribute success or failure in others to the people themselves. For example: "They failed because they didn't try hard enough," or "They failed because they just didn't know how to do that job." We tend to perceive the reason for our own failure as having to do with the situation, but we see the reason for failure in character.

Camille Wortman notes that when bad things happen (such as disaster or tragedy), we tend to attribute the cause to the person or group rather than the situation.[5] If a person gets mugged, we say: "That person should know better than to be on that street at night." Or, if a group fails to achieve an objective, we attribute the group's failure to lack of skills, performance, or motivation, rather than to the difficulties of the situation or changes in the environment that may have affected the group's ability to achieve the objective. People want to believe they are safe. Consequently, if we attribute the mugging to the environment, or the group's failure to difficult circumstances, then we must consider ourselves unsafe, too. So, rather than live with the belief that we may encounter the same problem, we tend to attribute the cause of the problem to the people affected by the problem. For example, after a company layoff, employees may say, "We got rid of the dead wood, so now we can be more productive." It is more threatening for employees to believe that good, competent workers were laid off than to believe the workers were unproductive and incompetent.

Melvin Lerner indicates that people want to believe in a just world. They want to believe that bad things happen to bad people and that good things happen to good people.[6] Many people confront this attribution process when they receive negative feedback.

> *When Julie reviewed her feedback, she became very silent. She stayed after the session to talk: "I don't know what I am going to do. It's obvious from this feedback that I will need to look for a new job." I asked to look at her feedback, expecting it to be terrible, but, although the feedback pointed out some clear problems, it wasn't that bad. Nevertheless, the feedback had convinced Julie, and she had moved past the situational attribution to the point that she believed herself to be totally responsible.*

Taking responsibility for feedback data is generally good, but Julie believed that bad things only happened to bad people. If she received bad feedback, she believed it meant that she was bad. However, good things and bad things happen to everybody. Yet we tend to blame the individual rather than look objectively at the situation.

Playing the Attribution Game

When people begin to understand the attribution process, they may conclude that their feedback is not correct. They think that rather than being the "truth," their feedback is full of attributions, packaged impressions, and halo effects. But such conclusions are misleading. The feedback we receive is typically accurate in that it reflects how people really feel about us and our performance. The attribution process helps to explain how people arrive at these feelings. For example, you might say your feedback is unfair because it doesn't accurately reflect the strengths of your group. But, as you understand more about the attribution process, you learn that this process has as much potential to work for you as it does to work against you.

> *Principle 12: The better you understand the attribution process, the more you can make it work to your advantage.*

Controlling the Attribution Process

1. Once people form their first impression, they strongly resist changing that impression. People tend to vigorously defend their first impressions. So, getting them to change those impressions is like causing an argument with themselves. To change those first impressions, we need some convincing arguments. One way to help people to change their attribution is to ask them for feedback and help in making a change. Find out which attributes are most important and which ones seem to be ignored.

2. People form a general impression and then rationalize specific characteristics and outcomes to fit their impression. Changing one characteristic may not be enough to change a general impression, especially when other outcomes continue to reinforce the general impression. When people or groups receive highly negative feedback, incremental improvement on a few issues frequently does not impact the overall impression. People with highly negative feedback need to consider, "What can we do to change the overall impression others have?" Changes that reshape initial or general impressions are referred to as frame-breaking changes. *(See Figure 2, demonstrating the difference between incremental and frame-breaking change.)*

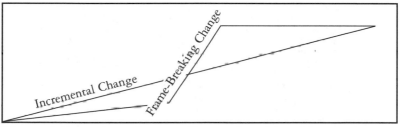

Figure 2: Incremental versus Frame-Breaking Change

3. People don't give equal attention to all attributes. Some count more than others. Understanding which outcomes or characteristics are most critical is an essential element in bringing about change.

4. Small changes in specific areas can have a significant positive impact on others and create a "halo" effect. Understanding how impressions are formed helps us and others form a more accurate perception of reality.

5. We tend to explain our personal or group failures as caused by environmental or situational factors. We might say, "The devil made me do it," or "We had a bad day," or "Circumstances changed." However, *we also tend to blame failure in others on the individual or group.* The reality is that both factors usually have at least some influence. Because others tend to blame failures on individuals or groups, rather than on circumstances, we need to inform others about adverse circumstances when failures are influenced by the situation rather than by a person.

> *Vern was a good engineer, but, as he put it, "I don't believe in beating my own drum. People should be able to figure out what I have done right and wrong without my having to explain all the details." Although Vern's attitude was noble, it significantly influenced the perceptions others had about his effectiveness.*
>
> *Vern had received some very negative feedback, which he felt was unfair. He later described a recent project in which he had encountered some difficult problems. "I suppose," he explained, "they blame all the problems of this project on me." However, Vern had never informed his boss or peers of the difficulties he was having with one of the suppliers, or that the client had made several late changes to the plans. Instead, Vern had learned, "In the absence of any other information, people will blame a failure on you."*

   6. People don't want to believe that the source of problems is your environment. When you or your group try to convince others that your problems are caused by the situation, others are not easily convinced. One reason may be that it sounds like an excuse. Another reason may be that people simply don't want to believe that the situation can be the cause of problems, because the world then becomes an unsafe and unpredictable place. Our natural tendency is to blame failure on the situation instead of objectively evaluating our performance.

Obtaining feedback helps to balance such tendencies with the possible attributions of others.

Notes for Chapter 3

1. Solomon E. Asch, "Forming Impressions of Personality." *Journal of Abnormal and Social Psychology* 41 (1946) 258-290.

2. Charles A. Dailey, "The Effects of Premature Conclusions upon the Acquisition of Understanding of a Person." *Journal of Psychology* 33 (1952), 133-152.

3. Alvin Scodel and Paul Mussen, "Social Perceptions of Authoritarians and Nonauthoritarians." *Journal of Abnormal and Social Psychology* 48 (1953), 181-184.

4. Harold H. Kelley, "The Process of Causal Attribution." *American Psychologist* 28 (1973), 107-128.

5. Camille B. Wortman, "Causal Attributions and Personal Control," in *New Directions in Attribution Research*, vol. 1., John H. Harvey, William John Ickes, and Robert F. Kidd, eds. Hillsdale, NJ: Lawrence Erlbaum Associates, 1976.

6. Melvin J. Lerner, "The Desire for Justice and Reactions to Victims," in *Altruism and Helping Behavior: Social Psychological Studies of Some Antecedents and Consequences,* Jacqueline R. Macaulay and Leonard Berkowitz, eds. New York: Academic Press, 1970.

4

WHY CHANGE?

Frequently, after people accept their feedback, they begin to wrestle with the question, "Why should I change?" Listed below are some of the attitudes we have encountered. Do you identify with any of them?

- "There are too many initiatives, new programs, and change efforts going on. I can't change everything."
- "I shouldn't be expected to jump and respond to every request."
- "Employees seem to grumble no matter what you do. If I fixed these issues they would just grumble about something else."
- "If others can't accept me with a few weaknesses, then that's their problem."
- "I can't make any changes until my boss and the rest of the organization decides to change."
- "I know my organization isn't perfect, but our strengths clearly outweigh our weaknesses. Why can't we just concentrate on our strengths."

If you identify with any of these thoughts, this chapter is for you! The larger an organization is, the harder it becomes

for people to believe that they can impact change in the organization or that they can affect change independent of the
rest of the organization. Most managers feel overwhelmed by
their duties and responsibilities.

In a recent survey, a company asked its employees to
respond to the statement, "My job is so demanding that it
causes problems in my personal life." The graph in Figure 3
shows how managers, supervisors, directors, vice presidents,
and chief executives responded much more negatively than
the remainder of the employee population.

	Disagree	Neutral	Agree
My job is so demanding that it causes problems in my personal/family life *(Company Average)*	61	20	19
Presidents/VPs/Directors	43	26	31
Managers/Supervisors	46	24	30
Asst. Managers/Non-Supervisors/ Independent Contributors	66	20	14
Administrative Support	79	12	9

0%   100%

Figure 3: Responses by Relative Position

The business world today has pushed people to ever higher
levels of productivity and efficiency. Many employees have
reached their limit. They have become tired of yet another
change when to them none of the change efforts seem to really
take hold and the only real impact the change effort has is to
provide people with more to do.

Feedback usually provides some good news and some bad
news. We find managers typically acknowledge their weaknesses, but they do not always try to face and improve them.
The most frequently mentioned comment when reviewing
feedback is, "I knew that we had a problem in this area."
Sometimes feedback comes as a big surprise, but people usually have known about their weaknesses for years. We often
ask people, "If you already knew about this, why didn't you

do something about it?" The answer is inevitably, "It didn't seem to be that important," or, "I just didn't want to do it." The problem with change isn't that organizations can't change; the problem is that they don't want the change badly enough. *(Figure 4: The dynamics of change with respect to commitment and difficulty.)*

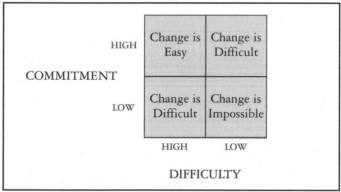

Figure 4: Commitment and Difficulty

Change is only easy when there is a high degree of commitment and a low degree of difficulty. When difficulty and commitment are both low, change is difficult; and, when commitment and difficulty are high, change is also difficult. But, when commitment is low and difficulty is high, change is impossible.

You've Got to Want It

You need to realize some things whenever you try to change anything about yourself or your organization. The first is that change won't just automatically happen. Simply acknowledging that a problem exists doesn't change the problem.

Principle 13: The first key to making a change is to increase your motivation and commitment to making the change.

Without high commitment, only the easiest issues can be resolved, and then only with some difficulty. The following sections provide some ideas to help you increase your commitment to change.

Performance Expectations Change over Time. Physiologist Walter B. Cannon wrote about the biological law of homeostasis. Homeostasis is the maintenance of equilibrium in a biological system. Cannon notes how the body maintains its balance through self-regulated internal mechanisms.[1]

Likewise, most people tend to migrate toward performance homeostasis. As people master their jobs, they typically try to achieve a more comfortable performance level. Because they have increased knowledge and skills, doing an effective job requires less effort and stress than when the job began. Most people strive for performance homeostasis. As people think about their performance, they typically justify this state by pointing out that they continue to perform at the same level, if not higher, than in years past.

The law of performance homeostasis predicts that most people would rather perform their jobs in a relaxed and comfortable state than in a stressed-out, exhausted state. Many people in organizations naturally move toward a more relaxed and comfortable state. The preference is the status quo rather than a new and different state.

Competition. Most of us believe we have to "pay our dues." But, once we have paid them, do we have to continue paying them? As we look back on our lives, most of us would think of school as a payment of dues. Perhaps the first few years of work serve as additional payment. We look forward to the time when we can generate excellent performance without much effort.

Things would work out fine except for one major problem—*The Competition!* While we rest on our laurels, having paid our dues already, someone is figuring out a way to do what your group does, only faster, cheaper, and with higher quality and better service. The reality of today's work place is that in order to survive, your group will have to change. The natural tendency of groups is to resist that change. Creating change in an organization to ensure survival is ultimately less stressful than the stress created by unemployment.

Many of today's workers do not incorporate competition into their basic philosophy about work. But, to survive, we must leave behind the desire to "take it easy." Organizations must encourage individuals and work groups to embrace continuous change, growth, and development. In the same way that exercise makes us strong, and preserves and enhances our lifestyle, the changes we make on the job can have dramatic positive effects. Leaders in organizations must step out front and foster the motivation necessary for people to change.

Average Isn't Good Enough. Most of us rate our performance on a continuum between "Bad" and "Excellent," and we tend to equate "Average" with "Pretty Good" or "Good Enough." So, if we rate our performance as "Bad," we feel a fair amount of motivation to change. But, if we rate our performance as "Average," we tend to accept that "Average" is good enough and we make few, if any, improvements.

As I work with organizations to help them measure performance and other criteria, I am frequently asked to help find the "bad work groups." After company work groups complete their evaluations, top management usually appears very surprised. Although we usually find one or two groups that are performing "badly," their performance is not typically poor enough to explain the sub-optimal performance of the company. Executives generally expect to find large numbers groups performing at disastrously bad paces that, if changed, would have a dramatic effect on company effectiveness. But, because of the small number of groups that could be considered "poor-performing," changing them would produce only small, incremental improvement in the company as a whole. To generate substantial improvement, the average-performing groups must also improve.

Many of us maintain a double standard in terms of our satisfaction with average performance. When we purchase a quality product, we expect exceptional performance, but we are often satisfied when our own performance is "about as good as everyone else." However, what we have discovered in our appetite for high-quality products, services, and personal performance is that *average is not good enough.* For a customer to notice the difference between one product and another, one has to stand out as distinct; it has to be exceptional. And, for company performance to excel it must also stand out, and be distinct and exceptional.

Average is never good enough to create excellence; instead it promotes mediocrity. Average performance can maintain loyal customers as long as everyone else in the industry is average and the demand for the company's products and services exceeds the supply. But, as companies begin to differentiate themselves by showing excellent performance in critical areas, average performance looks bad and customers migrate toward the exceptional.

Everything Counts. I find it amusing to go out to dinner with people who are on a diet. Some rigidly stick to their diets, but most, when tempted with a high-fat entrée or dessert, typically make one of the following excuses:

- This doesn't count if you eat before 6 p.m.
- This doesn't count if you eat it with your meal.
- This doesn't count if you exercise after you eat it.

One of the harsh realities of life (which most of us don't want to believe) is that *everything counts.* If mistakes or embarrassing experiences occur, they may be small, they may be forgotten, but they do count. Luckily, this phenomenon works both ways: Small, positive events also count.

As you consider the feedback received by you or your group, you might say to yourself that a particular issue was not that significant. You may say to yourself, "It doesn't count." But it does count. It may not count much looking at that particular weakness against all your strengths, and it may seem totally insignificant, but it counts. Highly effective organizations accept and believe this; average organizations ignore it.

Begin Where You Are. When an athletic team is in a losing slump, most coaches don't start at that point to introduce new, fancy, complicated plays. Instead, coaches work with their players on the basics. In football, for example, they review blocking and tackling rather than introducing the new "dipsy doodle." So often, groups go in search of a silver bullet to solve their problems while they continue to ignore the "fundamentals" that require immediate attention and improvement.

> *Workers in a large machine shop asked for advice on how to improve their performance. External consultants conducted interviews with several managers, who were asked what they thought the problems were in that location. Each manager had good, well-articulated ideas. But, when the managers were asked why they didn't simply work on the apparent problems, one manager answered, "They seem so simple. Surely there is some new, innovative solution for us that will create a fundamental change in the way we do business."*

These managers were looking for a silver bullet. The solution to their problems was to be found in the fundamentals. Looking beyond the actual problems is typical of many companies who are frustrated in their attempts to create higher performance. For these struggling companies, the fundamentals may seem simple-minded, but they are absolutely critical for success.

You Are Part of a Larger System. In our culture, we have a tremendous tendency to place blame. It starts at a very early age. If I ask my children who made a mess, they point the finger at another brother or sister. I am always amazed that when managers encounter complex and difficult problems, they frequently solve them by replacing somebody. The problem is still there, but now they have someone to blame.

I'm not only amazed by our tendency to blame others, but also by our willingness to take all the blame ourselves. "I blew it; I'm responsible," a manager once told me as we discussed a problem. It's as if life would be simpler for everybody if we could just take all the responsibility upon ourselves.

In reality, though, a group's performance problems are a function of three things:

1. The people in the group.

2. The environment or situation of the work group (the kind of work, the setting, the equipment, interaction with other groups, organizational culture, and so forth).

3. The people who interact with the work group (management, peers, and others in the organization).

Codependence

Codependence, a psychological theory currently used in helping alcoholics overcome their addiction, may offer some insights into resolving group performance problems. The basic notion of codependence is that people with drinking problems have those problems not only because of an inability to cope with alcohol, but also because of their relationships with others.

Although it is helpful to teach people to cope on their own with performance problems, it is usually more helpful to work on the whole environment. By helping us understand that much of the problem may have to do with interpersonal relationships and communication, the theory of codependence helps us not only with people who appear to have performance problems, but also with their support groups, including peers, work group members, managers, and so forth. As with alcoholism, understanding codependence helps managers and group members understand how their behavior may influence poor performance in the first place: When others in the work environment change, the probability of "poor performers" changing increases substantially.

Principle 14: Involving others in change efforts increases the probability that change will occur.

Typically, however, asking others for help is perceived as a weakness. Most of us view ourselves as "rugged individualists," making our own decisions, charting our own courses, and mapping out our own futures. We underestimate the influence of others on our own decisions and actions.

Notes for Chapter 4

1. Walter Cannon, *The Wisdom of the Body.* New York: Norton & Company, Inc., 1932.

5

DECIDING WHAT TO CHANGE

Several years ago, I arrived home very late from an out-of-town trip. As I slipped quietly into bed, I noticed a note on my pillow. I moved into the bathroom thinking that it was a love note from my wife. As I turned on the light in the bathroom, I read in large print on the cover page of the note:

"Things you can do to save our marriage."

This got my attention.

As I opened to the next page, I saw a list of 24 items. At the top of the list in the number one position was "Clean your office."

The next day, I got up and cleaned and organized my office. It took most of the day, but by the time I was finished it was perfect. My wife was impressed by my efforts, and so I thought I would not have to worry about doing the other 23 items.

I kept my office very clean for a few weeks and then asked my wife for some feedback. Her response was clear and to the point: "Nothing has changed," she said. "But what about the office?" I asked. With that, she just looked at me in disgust and walked off. What I have found out since then is that even though the appearance of my office is a frequent grumble for my wife, the cleanness of my office has almost no correlation with the quality of our marriage. My office can be disorganized and messy at the same time our marriage seems wonderful, or it can be very clean and organized even though our marriage is in turmoil.

I also found, however, that several other items on the list were directly and significantly correlated to the quality of our marriage. Some of these items included helping out more with the children and not being critical of her decisions and actions. I learned from this experience that I had been paying the most attention to the things others complained about the most or the loudest. This became my signal for learning what is most important. And frequently I have found that the issue at the top of the list is not necessarily the most important one to change.

Many work groups and organizations have similar experiences. Often, people find the issue that appears most negative and conclude it is the most important issue to change. This is faulty logic. Issues that are most negative or most complained about are simply the ones that are most noticeable. Evaluating what issues to change ought to be a completely separate decision-making process, independent from how negatively people react to issues.

In a perfect world, we would receive feedback on many issues and change everything. But, in the real world, people face limitations in how many issues they can successfully address at one time. A guaranteed way to fail in making change based on feedback is to try changing too many things at once. Our research shows that people, including work groups and organizations, cannot make five major changes at the same time. Whenever they try to change more than one, two, or three things at once, they end up making no changes at all.

Principle 15: The most critical skill in making a change based on feedback is deciding what specific issue to work on first.

Change is difficult. It requires focused effort and attention. Most change efforts don't occur in a vacuum. Organizations still have to complete their required work and continue to produce their products and services. However, focused effort on a few specific issues greatly improves the likelihood of success. So it's critical that you select the right issue to change.

In this chapter, you will learn how to prioritize issues from feedback and select issues to change that yield the most benefit.

Managing Expectations

When managers ask for feedback from employees, the employees expect the managers to take action on that feedback. It is helpful to establish the expectation up front that although employees may provide feedback on a variety of issues, managers' efforts might focus only on a few issues. To help manage these expectations, follow these five steps:

1. Thank employees who give you feedback.

2. Even though you may not be able to respond to every feedback issue, acknowledge that you received the feedback, and that it's valid.

3. Tell employees who give you feedback that you intend to focus on one, two, or three of the most critical issues.

4. Involve employees in analyzing feedback and creating plans for change.

5. Find a way to demonstrate that you are changing.

Even though employees would like their organizations to change everything based on their feedback, experience leads them to believe that little change will actually take place if too much is attempted. But, when the company makes a focused effort to change a few critical issues, employees are impressed and tend not to focus on issues not being changed.

Prioritizing Issues

The best approach for prioritizing issues is to list each of the issues and then consider how they rate against three different criteria: felt need, ease of change, and impact.

Felt Need. As you think about an issue from your feedback, ask yourself the extent to which you have a high, medium, or low felt need to change this issue. Don't confuse your felt need for change with the needs and desires of others. We change when we feel a strong enough need to change. If others think we need to change and we don't feel a need to change, then at best we can only talk about or act like we are changing, without actually changing.

In his extensive research on change, Gene Dalton reports that having a high felt need for change is the most important factor in predicting whether change will or will not occur. Dalton describes a classic example of the felt need of an alcoholic in the following scenario:

> *The wife of a man with a drinking problem asked him to go to Alcoholics Anonymous (AA). The man went to a counselor and indicated that he was there for the AA meeting. The counselor asked the man if he was an alcoholic. The man answered, "No, I don't think I'm an alcoholic, but my wife thinks I have a problem." The man then explained that he was there because his wife had asked him to come. The counselor replied, "Why don't you go drink some more because we can't do anything to help you until you think you have a problem."* [1]

For each of the issues for which you receive negative feedback, ask yourself which issues you most want to change. Make sure you separate your own desires from the desires of others. If your boss has placed a great deal of pressure on you or your group to change, determine whether your need to change is driven by you or by your boss.

Creating a Felt Need. The first step in bringing about a change is to create a felt need for change. As you think about the issues for which you have received feedback, perhaps you notice one issue for which others feel a high need for you to change, but you feel little or no need to change. How can you go about increasing your felt need?

The "not invented here" syndrome is the most fundamental hurdle keeping people from developing a strong need for change. You have the "not invented here" syndrome when you say things like, "My boss thinks our group needs to change this," or, "Other people think our group has a problem in this area." Your real felt need in these cases is not to change the problem, but to change other people's opinions about the problem.

One way to avoid the "not invented here" syndrome is to "reinvent" negative feedback. To reinvent feedback, take the feedback of others and place it in your own words, thoughts, and feelings. Start by examining how you look at a particular issue, and be totally honest with yourself in terms of the impact the issue is having on you and your group's performance, and on others. Try to understand why others become frustrated by the issue while you and your group do not. Is this an issue that negatively impacts others more than it does you?

If you can't reinvent feedback—taking ownership of the perceptions and feelings of others as your own—you will feel no need to change that issue. Your felt need for change may be lower than others' for two reasons: First, you don't understand the impact the issue is having on others; or second, you understand the impact, but you simply don't care as much as others do. It frequently helps to have frank, open discussions with others about the issues, especially the ones for which you continue to feel little or no need to change.

*After reviewing feedback from her direct reports,
Angela decided that her problem was not her behavior, but rather her staff's lack of understanding of
the situation. She arranged to have lunch with each
of them individually to talk about their feedback
and help them understand her situation.*

*At lunch Angela would thank each member of
her team for his or her feedback, and then she would
describe her situation. Her employees listened
patiently to her, and then, one by one, they informed
Angela that they had been well aware of her situation. But this fact did not change the relevance of
their feedback. They reinforced to Angela that she
needed to change her own behavior, even though the
situation made it difficult. By the time Angela had
taken four of her direct reports to lunch, her need for
change was high enough for her to pursue the issue
and make some changes.*

Your need for change is affected by two perspectives:
First, a clear understanding of how the issue negatively
affects you and your associates or other groups (the "push"),
and second, an understanding of the positive impact of making a change (the "pull"). Most often, we focus our attention
on the "push," or the negative impact of the issues. But the
"pull" can provide even more motivation. If you understand
only the negative impact of your behavior but have no sense
for the positive impact of change, you will have less motivation
to change and therefore have a lower felt need. By focusing on
the "pull," you begin to consider the benefits of making a
change. This change of focus can turn guilt into proactivity
and frustration into action.

Ease of Change. Some issues are easier to change than
others. In planning a change process, select at least one issue
you know will be easy to change. This not only gives you

confidence in your ability to change, but it sends a positive signal to others that you are responding to their feedback. *(See Figure 5, which provides some helpful guidelines in judging the relative ease of change.)*

ISSUES	EASE OF CHANGE
Equipment and Resources	
Staff	
Skill Development	Easier
Systems and Processes	
Structure	
Individual Behavior	Harder
Stereotypes and Prejudices	
Values and Company Culture	

Figure 5: Relative Ease of Change

For example, equipment and resources are generally easier to change than values and company culture.

Clarity and Difficulty. After we form our overall impression of a person or group, we adjust our feedback on various characteristics to fit the overall impression. We also use a "packaging" approach (a general impression to attribute a broader set of characteristics) to provide feedback. Frequently, however, we make attributions based on a few specific behaviors and determine that someone has a certain personality characteristic.

Suppose you are the manager of a group, and you commit to having a personal performance review with each group member at least twice per year. During the year you have a few informal chats with group members on specific projects. In your mind, you are conducting personal performance reviews. Your employees, on the other hand, believe that personal performance reviews should be more formal. They expect either you or themselves to fill out a form and to discuss a rating with you. After a company-wide survey, you receive negative feedback from your team. One survey item reads, "My immediate supervisor is honest in dealing with the work group," and another reads, "My performance is reviewed with me regularly." Your rating on both items is poor.

Dishonesty is a personal characteristic that is very difficult to change. On the other hand, not giving people formalized feedback on a regular basis is easier to change. Most of us rarely clarify how we form our conclusions. Most of the time, we provide feedback based on our overall impressions, and packaged bundles of traits that fit those impressions, rather than on the specific behaviors that led us to our conclusions. Clarity regarding what needs to be changed can significantly improve a person or group's chance of changing.

Things Versus People. Another consideration in rating the difficulty of change is this:

Principle 16: Issues dealing with things are much easier to change than those dealing with people.

For example, correcting a "bug" in a software program is easier to change than managing the conflict between members of a work group. Changing things is easier than changing people for two reasons: First, we have much more control over things (things don't resist or reject changes, as people often do); and second, we are more skillful at working with things than with people. But changes that involve others don't need to be more difficult if we are skillful in the way we deal with people.

Relative Impact. We tend to think effective organizations have excellent skills in every area—that they are "excellent at everything." But, after studying profiles of many highly rated organizations, we find that the "excellent at everything" notion doesn't hold true. Profiles show that while the most respected companies may score highly in some characteristics, they score average and even poorly in others. When we asked one executive of a highly rated company about his low scores, he responded, "We don't pay much attention to that stuff. It just doesn't seem that critical."

Also, when we look at profiles of low-rated companies, we don't find them to be terrible at everything. Their profiles show poor performance in one or two critical areas, but poor performance in critical areas has a negative halo effect on other areas.

The most critical question in prioritizing issues is: "If you were to change one issue, which one would make a significant difference in the overall performance of the group in terms of its ability to produce its core product or service?" Many changes are nice for morale, but once the dust settles, people in the group often wonder, "Is there any relationship between change in this area and improvement of our ability to accomplish our mission?" Whenever you make changes on high-impact issues, others notice big changes in bottom-line performance. But, when you make changes on low-impact issues, others either do not notice the changes or they do not see them as very important.

A few high-impact changes may have a performance lag. They can have long-term impact, but in the short run they often are not noticed. For example, employee career development issues often have a performance lag. Losing high-performance employees because they see no long-term career opportunities, however, can lead to a stagnant company performance over the long term.

To evaluate the relative impact of changing different issues, consider these two questions:

1. Which issues are most important?

2. How effective does our organization need to be on those issues?

Which Issues Are Most Important? ✓

To assess relative impact of making a change, you first need to distinguish between essential, necessary, and nonessential skills, knowledge, and activities.

Essential Skills, Knowledge, and Activities are those which, if executed well, lead to high performance in the organization.

Necessary Skills, Knowledge, and Activities are those that need to be performed and are required of the job, but they are not as strongly linked to perceived high performance. These areas may be helpful for high performance and often require good or average execution, and, in fact, they can't be ignored. But doing an exceptional job on them will not create exceptional performance for the organization.

Holding regular meetings is a good example. Most work groups meet regularly to share information, make decisions, and build team unity. Suppose employees in your group suggest that you meet more often. Responding to that feedback, you decide that, rather than meeting once a month as has been the case, you will now hold meetings every day. Although having regular meetings is necessary for most groups, having daily meetings will probably not improve your group's performance. In fact, daily meetings may even reduce group performance. Your next employee survey might read, "We can't get any work done because we're always in meetings."

Nonessential Skills, Knowledge, and Activities are things that are not required, nor are they linked to high performance. These things may be important to you or to the execution of other jobs, but they are not important to your organization's core mission. Most groups feel they have very few nonessential assignments, but in reality, most groups have many. We may feel a particular activity is important, but executives and other groups fail to see its value. For some organizations, nonessential activities take the form of bureaucracy or difficult paper work, sustained by tradition or habit, making work difficult to accomplish. Up to 50 percent of the activities in most organizations add no value.

Activity Analysis

Make a list of the various skills and activities required of your group. After you make the list, classify each as "essential," "necessary," or "nonessential." Most groups classify 80 to 90 percent of their lists as essential, but since they are not completely clear about how "essential" differs from "necessary," they disperse their effectiveness, spending equal effort on both essential and necessary areas.

We find that bosses and peers from other groups frequently are even less clear about the distinction. If you ask them what is essential, they tend to respond that everything is essential. We can gain greater clarity through study and negotiation, rather than by simply asking. The process starts when you decide what is essential.

Select five activities from your list that you feel are most essential. To help you make the selection, ask yourself the following questions:

1. Which of these skills or activities could we perform at an average or good level and still be achieve top performance overall?

2. If we only did one or two of these things well, which one would make the biggest difference or have the most significant impact on our group's performance?

3. Which activities or skills do people notice and recognize when we do them well?

4. Which one or two activities would our boss classify in the "nonessential" category.

5. Which skill or activity is most highly correlated with our group's ability to carry out our core mission or objective?

6. If we were to stop doing one of these things, what impact would it have on our ability to achieve our core mission or objective?

Every group and organization must figure out what it takes to improve its own bottom line. Most jobs have a central mission or activity along with many secondary activities. Carefully consider which activities really contribute to the bottom line and which are secondary. Groups must clearly define what is essential for them, and then determine how best to deliver that essential assignment. You may discover a significant difference between what you think is important and what others perceive as important. Focusing your efforts on activities that make a difference is critical. Keep in mind that in some organizations group performance is judged in terms of activities rather than results.

Reach an agreement with your boss and peers about which activities are essential. Frequently, this consensus comes through negotiation. Other times it comes when you or your group accept the views of others about what is important.

The end result of this exercise is that you clarify which activities are essential, necessary, and nonessential. Now link your feedback to the list: Often you will see a one-to-one correlation, such as in the following example:

> *The directors of a large manufacturing company prioritized their essential activities. At the top of their list was "Control costs." As the directors reviewed employee survey results, they looked for the most negative issues. According to the survey, the most negative result had to do with the company's endless bureaucracy and red tape that made efficient work difficult. The correlation quickly became apparent: By reducing bureaucracy, the company could increase efficiency and reduce costs.*

Other times, the links are more ambiguous:

> *The organization also had an aggressive plan for creating semi-autonomous teams. By empowering the people in each work group and asking the teams to be self-managing, the company planned eventually to*

*reduce the number of supervisors and managers,
allowing for a substantial cost savings. But, unless
the teams learned collaborative decision-making and
self-management, this goal could never be achieved.
Therefore, "teamwork" was selected as a critical issue
because, once again, it would lead to reduced costs.*

Whenever feedback issues are not directly linked to one skill or activity, look for one or two issues that have the most significant correlation. The following table will help you establish the correlation between essential, necessary, and nonessential areas and the feedback you receive. After completing the table, you will find it easy to assign different levels of importance to each of the feedback items. You may need more time to complete this table if you still need to negotiate some of the importance levels with others.

List of Skills/ Knowledge/ Activities	Essential	Necessary	Non-Essential	Correlation with Feedback Issues
_____	_____	_____	_____	_____
_____	_____	_____	_____	_____
_____	_____	_____	_____	_____
_____	_____	_____	_____	_____
_____	_____	_____	_____	_____
_____	_____	_____	_____	_____
_____	_____	_____	_____	_____
_____	_____	_____	_____	_____
_____	_____	_____	_____	_____
_____	_____	_____	_____	_____
_____	_____	_____	_____	_____
_____	_____	_____	_____	_____
_____	_____	_____	_____	_____
_____	_____	_____	_____	_____
_____	_____	_____	_____	_____
_____	_____	_____	_____	_____

Table 1

How Good Is Good Enough?

A cost-benefit analysis for a manufacturing process showed that as the costs of purifying a material increased, the benefit derived from the strength and appearance of the final product decreased. Organizational performance can be viewed in the same light. Sometimes good performance in one skill is all that is necessary. Absolute excellence would not produce any noticeable impact.

An organization's performance and effectiveness are usually judged in comparison to that of other organizations. Your group's performance relative to others may be described in three ways:

Competitive advantage: excellent performance compared to others, above average.

Parity: performance at about the same level as others, average.

Competitive disadvantage: inadequate performance compared to others, well below average.

If a particular issue is essential and your performance gives you a competitive advantage, you should work to maintain that level of effectiveness. If your performance is average, you should work to improve your effectiveness. If you feel you have a competitive disadvantage, you should work to make major changes.

Before you evaluate your group's performance by these three definitions, first determine the level of perceived importance that others, particularly bosses, have assigned. Performance that you would describe as on parity with others, and which you find to be necessary in terms of importance (but not essential) should be maintained. Performance that gives you a competitive disadvantage, with a necessary level of importance, needs to be improved. However, having a competitive disadvantage on nonessential issues makes no difference to your performance, and you shouldn't invest much energy in improving performance in these areas. *(Figure 6 shows how to combine importance ratings with the level of effectiveness rating.)*

		IMPORTANCE		
		Essential	Necessary	Nonessential
	Competitive Advantage	Maintain	OK	OK
ORGANIZATIONAL EFFECTIVENESS	Average Performance	Improve	Maintain	OK
	Competitive Disadvantage	Major Change	Improve	Maintain

Figure 6: Effectiveness/Importance Rating

Prioritization Worksheet

Use the following table to list the most negative issues from your group's feedback. Then rate the items "high," "medium," or "low," according to felt need, ease of change, and the item's relative impact.

List of Issues	Felt Need	Ease of Change	Relative Impact

Table 2

After you complete the prioritization worksheet, you should have a much better idea of what to work on. As you select issues to work on, consider the following criteria:

1. Don't select more than three issues to work on at once. In fact, for best results, select only one issue. You will find tremendous power in focusing all your energy for change on fewer issues. Although you may be tempted to select more than three, don't fall into the trap of taking on too much.

2. If the three issues you have selected are all difficult to change, consider selecting one issue that is easier to change. Look for a "quick win" with one issue. This not only sends a positive message to others, but it also provides you with some needed confidence.

3. Don't select an issue that others want changed more than you want to change yourself. Until your felt need matches others' felt needs, the odds of making a lasting change are significantly reduced.

4. Find one essential issue that will give you a competitive advantage.

Notes for Chapter 5

1 Gene W. Dalton, Louis B. Barnes, and Abraham Zaleznik, *The Distribution of Authority in Formal Organizations.* Boston, MA: Division of Research, Harvard Business School, 1968, Chapter 5: "Change in Organizations" (Reprinted Boston, MA: MIT Press, 1973).

6

CREATING CHANGE IN ORGANIZATIONS

Creating change in organizations is difficult. Both executives and employees resist unintended or chaotic changes. Leaders work hard to create stable systems, processes, and employees because consistency, order, and predictability are needed in organizations. Both employees and leaders count on things being the same way tomorrow as they were today. In many ways, most changes seem unneeded since apparently we want to create organizations that don't change.

On the other hand, organizations face a world that is quickly changing. To survive, an organization must adapt. Organizations that are not able to make necessary adjustments will no longer exist in the future. Any organization with an ability to change quickly and efficiently in desired ways will have a substantial competitive advantage.

Change efforts are often difficult for organizations. Employees do not always cooperate. Previous changes once sold as benefits to employees generally turned out to be benefits only for a few, while the rest were left skeptical and cynical, or "downsized." Change, by its very nature, creates the possibility of losing something. It also creates the possibility of winning something. The change process is usually unsure, unstable, and comes associated with some risk. Many employees would rather be secure with what they have than risk losing something. Change is inevitably messy. The process places people in unique situations where they don't know exactly what to do. Often, change requires people to perform new jobs requiring different skills. Typically, the change process brings confusion, and people generally don't like confusion.

As managers and employees begin the process of change, they sometimes believe anything is possible. "If other organizations have done this, why can't we?" And, although many organizations have gone through incredible changes, some organizations can handle the stress, but others can't. Something my father used to say captures what I'm referring to: "You can't make a silk purse out of a sow's ear." He would use that quote whenever I would attempt crazy things like trying to impress girls with our family car. The car was definitely a "sow's ear," and all my girlfriends knew it.

Organizations, like people, develop differently. They have different skills, personalities, attitudes, and abilities. An individual may desire to become a great athlete. Hard work, determination, practice all contribute to improving one's performance, but being great is more often a function of all the above combined with genetics. Physical size, coordination, mental ability, and other inherent traits usually make the final difference. In the same way, many organizations are limited by their genetic makeup. A dramatic change for one organization might be quite simple and only take a few months. But, for another organization it might take years, and even then it may be done only moderately well.

A variety of skills and processes can facilitate organizational change. However, the skills and processes that best facilitate change are not the same for all organizations.

Principle 17: An organization's history and experience help determine which skills and processes will be most useful in a successful change effort.

In this chapter I present a variety of approaches that can help organizations facilitate change. Often, to successfully implement changes, several of these approaches may have to be used. These processes and skills can be thought of as levers, and the more levers an organization employs, the more likely it will be able to succeed in its change initiatives.

1. Finding the Real Problem

A large organization had just completed its first organizational climate survey. The results were presented to the company's top managers first, and then to all other managers and supervisors. The results showed a strong positive climate, as well as several negative issues. One of the most negative issues from the data was "collaboration." Items such as the following were responded to negatively:

- "Many groups are competing against each other for equipment, people, money, or recognition to the detriment of the company."
- "Because work groups are not collaborating, the result is duplicated effort."
- "Company resources are wasted because work groups don't work together."

The feedback was generally accepted as true for the whole company. At a meeting in which the survey results were shared with all managers in the company, the president stood up and made an impassioned plea for the managers to make improvements and changes in collaboration. It felt like something positive

was going to happen. But, after 18 months had passed, another
survey showed that collaboration actually had become more negative than it had been. Once again, the president stood and
appealed to the managers to improve. This time, he seemed even
more impassioned, more focused. The managers felt terrible. They
felt they had let their president down. They wanted to change and
thought they had done better this time. They left the meeting
again committing to do all they could to personally solve this
problem. But again, after 18 months, collaboration was still a
problem for the company.

The following represents a typical top management feedback
meeting:

- Present survey results.
- Top management agrees on the most important issues
  to change.
- Everyone agrees and becomes enthusiastic about making some change.
- Group leaders say, "I am personally committed to
  changing this issue, and I hope everyone here is just as
  committed."
- No one says they're not committed.
- Group leaders say, "Well then, let's do it! What's the
  next agenda item?"

Most executives don't have the time or the patience to
unravel complex organizational problems. You might argue
that it isn't even their job to do so. Whether it is or isn't their
job, it seems that whenever organizational feedback is presented to executives, the president or division leader typically
follows with an enthusiastic speech. The leader encourages
people to make significant changes based on the feedback.
Group members then nod in approval, and the organization
goes forth with its business.

If you talk to executives one month after this event, they
still remember the feedback and the speech and are quite sure

someone in the company is doing something about it. They may even remind their direct reports, and the direct reports nod and say, "right." Each is sure that someone else is working on the problem. Many of them, in turn, share the reminder with their own direct reports, who likewise agree to work on the issue. As obvious as it seems from this apparent satire, the reason organizations don't solve their problems is because they never actually work on the problem.

The best approach for making change on issues raised by climate surveys is to include a root-cause analysis in the survey process. As before, top executives confirm the top survey issues, but, before they give their speech, they should indicate the next step is to assign a separate group to prepare a root-cause analysis and generate action plans for the executive team's approval.

2. Making Change a Priority

Organizational Erosion. Change initiatives in organizations can be compared to rocks. These rocks experience organizational erosion. Organizational erosion is much quicker than natural erosion. For example, a person could generate a very large change-initiative rock, and within a month the rock would be half that size. Within three months the rock would be a mere pebble and hardly noticeable among all the other pebbles in the organization. You can't stop this erosion; you can only increase the size of the rocks. For change-initiative rocks to survive, you must generate huge rocks. So, the first question to ask is, "Is this change really that important?" In other words, can you justify making this change initiative huge. If the rock is only large or medium size, it probably will not survive unless it can be implemented in a few short months. Change-initiative rocks that are large and never get fully eroded (or implemented) create significant distractions to the organization. They form obstacles and leave little room for other change-initiative rocks. Organizations are better off not

being disrupted with change initiatives that are never implemented.

Principle 18: Organizations cannot stop to implement changes; they must change while they continue to execute.

Organizations have an endless supply of activities: getting work done, training employees, maintaining and
improving systems and processes, meeting customer expectations, and, of course, conducting meetings, meetings, and
more meetings. When it comes to change initiatives, organizations must ask, "Can this initiative compete with all the
other events and activities going on in the organization?" It
seems each organization is engaged in a football game that
only ends when the organization is out of business. You can
call time-out, but only a few times. You must get the attention of the players during those time-outs, help them
improve the way they are executing. They need a new vision,
a plan, a reason to change, and the motivation to do so.

Once you determine that a particular change initiative
can hold its own with all the other activities and initiatives
going on in the organization, you then need to build the case
for change in the organization. The process of building a case
involves the following steps:

Preparing the Case for Change. Just as lawyers prepare
cases before they go to court, you must prepare your case for
change. The following questions need persuasive arguments:

- Why does the organization need to change?
- What will happen if it doesn't change?
- What will the organization look like after the change is com-
  pleted?
- Who will be affected by the change?
- How will the company go about changing?

- Who in the organization needs to be committed to this change for it to succeed?

  Communicating the Case for Change. After preparing your case for change, the next step is to communicate the change to those who need to know. Typically the communication process needs the following elements:

  - Build support with key stakeholders.
  - Occur more than once.
  - Use several different mediums such as speeches, articles in company newsletters, e-mail messages, training programs, and so forth.
  - Repeat the message to stakeholders and others involved in making the change.
  - Deliver a consistent message.
  - Remain focused.

3. Building Support

Organizational change rarely occurs on one person's effort alone. Any change that requires cooperation from others absolutely requires support from the people who will be cooperating. Building a broad support base for organizational change is usually more difficult than it seems. I frequently see managers talk to their direct reports about change efforts. The direct reports typically express interest, excitement, and personal commitment when the managers describe the change to be made. The managers then believe the change should be fairly simple and straightforward. However, when it comes time for individuals in the group to change, they often resist changing. Most direct reports have learned the art of acting interested and committed. Also, even when direct reports are genuinely interested and committed, they often lose momentum when they realize the extent to which the change will affect them personally.

Principle 19: Before announcing any change, managers should build a broad support base for the change, including input from stakeholders at various organizational levels.

Most people underestimate the difficulty of building support. They make bold announcements before others have heard anything about the change. They expect others to be as excited and committed to the change as they, themselves, are. Managers typically assume that just because they think something is a good idea, others will naturally agree. For this reason, such a bold beginning to a difficult change process often ends in failure. The more support that can be lined up prior to announcing a new change initiative, the higher the probability will be that a significant change can be successfully implemented.

Gaining support for a change effort can be approached in many different ways. For example, the way you came to be committed to a change effort may not be a way that is as effective for others. People differ in how they become committed. Understanding the different ways people are motivated, and then applying the right motivation to the right people, will improve your ability to gain commitment.

4. Building Commitment

You can build support and commitment using proven tools.

Honesty and Sincerity. The most universal tool for gaining support is honesty and sincerity. If people believe and trust you, they will more likely believe in and trust your change efforts. Businesspeople are tempted almost daily to bend the facts or not to disclose all the information in a straightforward manner. Although there sometimes may be short-term reasons to use manipulative strategies, people will find out the truth in the long run and will then be much more cautious about trusting you.

Logic. Many people can be motivated to change through logical arguments. Laying out a clear picture of current reality versus the future state of things, illustrating the facts, and showing clear examples often leads to getting many people on board for the proposed change process. A good theory that can be proven is often a very useful tool. Using logic and rational arguments is probably the most common approach for gaining commitment from others. But this strategy does not work for everyone. Good logic, a well-reasoned theory, and rational arguments need to be used in addition with other tools for fostering commitment.

Friendship and Loyalty. Friendship and loyalty can be used to build support in two ways: First, your friends are more likely to listen to you and trust what you say. Also, they generally are more open to your logic; second, you can sometimes ask friends to cooperate even though they have reservations. I like to look at this tool as a kind of checking account for personal favors. Through your associations with that person, you build up a line of credit based on mutual integrity and loyalty, and now you are making a withdrawal of some of that credit. Keep in mind that people tend to keep good track of the balance, and as it gets close to zero they become less willing to let you make withdrawals.

Bottom-Line Financial Impact. It's easy for employees to forget that all organizations must deliver results, stay within budgets, and generate a reasonable profit. Some change efforts are rolled out without any apparent connection to the bottom line. Making a clear connection between proposed change efforts and their impact on the bottom line often helps people build commitment and support. Other times, employees need to be clear about the financial consequences of not implementing changes. Creating a realistic picture of a negative financial downside because change initiatives are ignored can also help generate commitment.

Reward/What's in It for Me? Punishment and rewards are two effective methods of changing behavior. Having clear cause-effect relationships for specific performance standards and outcomes can have dramatic impact on support. People may argue your logic or the reality of the bottom line, but when you reward desired outcomes many people become committed. Keep in mind that there are many different rewards besides money. Some people want job security more than money; others want freedom to work without close supervision, and still others want promotions or opportunities for challenging work.

Desire to Win. Good coaches help prepare their teams for big games. They help teams understand the strengths and weaknesses of the competition and then practice hard to defend themselves. Although sports analogies are frequently overused, helping people become enthusiastic about their work stimulates higher performance. Conflicts with competitors can serve to unite people who previously had fought only against each other in the company. Unions and management, research and manufacturing, or sales and production can become committed and united against a common foe.

The Support Test. A good test for whether you have enough support is to sit back and see how others in the organization push an initiative forward. If, when you back off, the initiative quickly loses momentum, you have not created enough support. When you have created sufficient support you will notice that others in the organization begin to drive the changes harder and more consistently than you. Also, if others become highly supportive, change initiatives typically evolve from their original concepts.

5. Keeping a Clear Vision

When I was 12 years old, I had a job working for my uncle on his farm. One Saturday, early in the spring, my uncle asked me to come with him in the truck to his grain field. He had been plowing the field but had another commitment and was going to teach me to plow. Sitting at one end of the field was a huge Caterpillar tractor. Actually, the tractor wasn't that large, but at age twelve I couldn't think of anything more fun that driving a Caterpillar.

To teach me, my uncle drove as I sat on the fender and he explained the levers and buttons. We then plowed up one row and down another. He asked if I could do it, and I replied, "No problem." He stepped down from the Caterpillar and let me take the controls. He stood by and told me to try the next row on my own. I pulled down on the throttle, the diesel engine revved, and I felt the power as I let up on the clutch. I was totally focused on staying right on the edge of the previous furrow. I looked down by the front track of the Caterpillar and made occasional adjustments to make sure I stayed the appropriate distance from the plowed ground.

When I finished the row, my uncle stopped me and had me step off the tractor to look at my furrow. His furrow was a perfectly straight line all the way down the row, but mine was a wavy line. I had made many corrections to stay the appropriate distance from the plowed ground. My uncle congratulated me on doing a pretty good job, but then he said I needed to make one change: "Don't look down at the ground right in front of the Caterpillar; instead, look at a fence post or rock at the end of the field that's in line with where you want to end up." I followed his advice, and the next time I plowed a straight furrow.

To me, this story serves as a great example of the value of having a clear vision. I see so many employees who execute their jobs while looking at the ground right in front of their

feet. They understand what others want them to do, but they
are not clearly focused on the end point. A vision is a clear
picture of a desired future state. The purpose of a vision is to
help employees set their direction and to provide a general
heading. Vision is different from planning. Vision is designed
to produce change, while a plan provides order for how
things are to be accomplished. Having a good plan with no
vision is like looking at the ground in front of the tractor.

Real change often begins as a recognition that a problem
exists. Communication then can begin. People soon become
clear about what they don't want. This is an important step in
the process, but more important is the clear vision of where to
go. Effective visions have the following characteristics:

- A vision is a destination, a place we want to go and not
  a place we want to avoid.
- Clarity is needed not only about what the destination is,
  but also about what it is not. Often it is just as important
  to describe where we are not going as where we want to go.
- Visions must be visual. People must be able to see the
  picture in their minds.
- Most visions begin as distant objects that can be seen, but
  they become much clearer and focused as you get closer.
- Visions are simple. A complex vision is difficult to clarify and often leads people in multiple directions.
- Clear visions can be communicated in less than five
  minutes.
- Exciting visions are mentioned often.
- Visions should be simplified to make them more realis-
  tic and attainable.
- Powerful visions often balance the interests of impor-
  tant constituencies.
- The best visions are consistent with other initiatives
  and strategies. If a new vision sends a different message

than a previous vision, employees need to understand which is the correct message and why it has changed.

6. Communicating the Change

One of the most significant keys for implementing organizational change is communicating the change to employees throughout the organization. We often underestimate the need for constant communication, perhaps because we feel like we are repeating ourselves. This is true, but consider how we raise our children: Although we would like to believe that when we tell them something they will remember it for the rest of their lives, we learn by experience that we must find ways to reinforce important messages. When people don't hear messages for a long time they tend to forget the messages are important. A few keys for effectively communicating change include:

- *Talk about the change at every opportunity.* When implementing a change, bring it up as frequently and as often as possible.
- *Rely on face-to-face, one-on-one communication.* Change starts at the grass roots, not in large meetings or company newsletters. Describing a change to a small group, face to face, provides the opportunity for dialog.
- *Use all available communications vehicles.* Get the message out and then continue to repeat the message out in multiple forms and formats.
- *Speak more with front-line supervisors and employees than with senior management.* Senior managers need to be committed to making a change, but frequently they're already on board. Assuming the next level will fall in line with change efforts without any discussion or involvement is naive.
- *Focus on activities, not attitudes.* Most change efforts begin with people who are not 100 percent on board. Typically, you hear negative comments, criticisms, and

critiques. Focus on activities (what people are doing) rather than on attitudes (what people are saying). Attitudes soon fall in line with behaviors and activities.

- *Describe what should happen over the long term.* In the beginning of change efforts, people often focus on activities or behaviors that need to be different. But focusing attention on these factors takes energy away from long-term visions. Remember, keep watching the fence post.

- *Communicate with energy.* You are responsible not only to let people know where the company is going, but for getting them excited about going there. Excitement is contagious. I call this the Broadway dilemma. Most actors on Broadway want to star in a hit play, but the problem is that hit plays seem to go on for years. How can actors perform the same roles over and over, day after day, and still maintain enthusiasm for their job? The answer involves one of the secrets of change: To be successful, you must learn to maintain the same enthusiasm the first, the fiftieth, and the one-hundredth time you discuss your vision.

- *Communicate a sense of urgency.* Letting people know that the change you are planning is important and needs special attention is critical to managing a successful change effort.

- *Articulate a feasible way to achieve the vision.* All great journeys begin with the first step. Some visions paint a clear picture of the destination but provide only a sketchy map of how to get there. Communicate where to start. Communicate the first few months of activities and then tie them in to the final destination.

- *Articulate the vision stressing the values of the audience.* People have different motives that influence their willingness to change. Clarify for different groups how a change ought to be communicated. Avoid selling or manipulation strategies; instead, describe change initiatives in language that fits your audience.

7. *Moving from General to Specific*

Change efforts often begin as very general recommendations. For example, we might say:

- "We need to improve the way we communicate."
- "Quality needs to be better."
- "We are not serving customers the way we should."

These general recommendations are great as a starting place for change. If, however, the suggestion for change remains general, then nothing is likely to change.

Gene Dalton found that to change, people must adjust their change plans from general terms to specific. General plans rarely lead to actual change because general plans and goals supply no specific actions to take. In fact, when organizations have only a general goal for change, no one knows how to take action to achieve the goal. Specific plans set the goals in motion and provide detailed, specific actions that lead to goal accomplishment.[1]

By keeping change plans general, organizations never have to change anything. The following conversation I had with my son, Brandon, about his grades, represents this idea:

"Son, what are your goals for your grades in school next semester?"

"I'm going to get better grades, Dad."

"How much better?"

"Oh, I don't know. But, you know, better than last semester."

"Does that mean a straight-A average?"

"No, not straight-As, Dad, but I'll do better. Can I go to Ben's house now?

"First, tell me your goal. How much better are your grades going to be?"

"Just better, Dad. Why can't you just trust me to do better? Can I go to Ben's house now?"

By keeping the change goal general, Brandon didn't have to commit to anything. General goals do not lead to any specific behaviors, such as studying for three hours per night, having homework done before any other activities, turning in all assignments, doing well on all tests, doing extra-credit assignments, and retaking tests and assignments that result in low grades. Therefore, the odds of achieving the goal are greatly reduced.

General goals let us avoid the hassles of reality. But, by creating specific goals, we force ourselves to consider what it actually will take to change. Part of the movement from general goals to specific goals is deciding what we will do.

8. Learning from the Best

As organizations attempt significant change, they often find it difficult to know how to proceed and what to avoid. In most cases, the same changes have been made successfully by other organizations, and it can be helpful to benchmark against those organizations to help you understand what it takes. Many companies in the same industry will not allow specific benchmarking, but you can sometimes find organizations that are not competing with you for customers and that have been through similar experiences and have perhaps mastered some key skills for making a successful transition.

> *A petrochemical reseller was experiencing a significant shift in how its customers were purchasing products from distributors. To help the company understand how other organizations had handled significant changes in buying patterns and the effects of new technology, the company studied banks. With the influx of automated tellers, and with increased competition from other financial institutions, banks have had to make significant changes in how they worked with customers and new technology. The*

petrochemical company's study was helpful in guiding its distributor through the complicated technological options and their implications.

Another company focused on improving its speed. The company defined "speed" as the time it took from taking an order to having the product installed. The benchmarking team decided to look at the difference between a typical garage and a Q-Lube station in terms of the speed required for a typical oil change. The garage required people to leave their cars for the entire day, but Q-Lube was able to change the oil and lubricate the car in 10 to 15 minutes while people waited. The Q-Lube had specialized to the point that it only changed oil, while the garage handled a variety of repairs, many of which required lengthy processes. As the benchmarking team studied these companies, it quickly became evident that to improve speed, the company would need to reduce the product options offered to customers.

Our experience with benchmarking suggests that many companies are willing to take some time and share their learning with others. This can be an inexpensive way to obtain a great deal of knowledge quickly.

9. Defining Feedback Positively

In their book, *When Smart People Fail,* Carole Hyatt and Linda Gottlieb discuss the problems some successful people have when they encounter failure. When "failure makes us feel powerless and like a victim," change does not occur. They recommend that you "reinterpret your story" by casting your feedback in a more positive light, one in which you have more control.[2]

Principle 20: Redefining negative feedback in a positive light creates increased motivation to change.

Engineers at a production plant were experiencing some significant reliability problems with the plant. Breakdowns would bring down the entire plant and cost as much as one million dollars per day. As maintenance engineers met to discuss the plant's reliability, it was clear that they felt at least partially responsible for the problem, but they also blamed many others who they felt contributed to the plant's poor reliability record. The plant was old, and cheap parts had been purchased to replace parts that were failing. Additionally, the problem-solving sessions held to discuss the breakdowns had typically turned into name-calling sessions, and few problems were solved in the meetings. Morale was low, people were frustrated, and nothing was changing. No one denied the problem, but no positive actions were being taken.

When things go wrong, we naturally assume defensive positions that do not facilitate change. Reviewing the problem, focusing on who was responsible and what action should be taken against whom, tends to paralyze people. The vision for change needs to be cast in a positive light. People need to know what to do, not what to avoid. In the above example, the plant was able to identify three immediate actions that needed to take place. People were organized, plans were made, and action was begun. There was very little resistance to the new programs, and they were easily implemented.

10. Connecting Change with Company Culture

A company culture is the organization's way of thinking and behaving. Within the company it seems natural and is hardly noticeable. Typically, company culture is unwritten, but it represents policy that can be very consistent and difficult to change.

A government contractor had built a factory to make computer chips. Because of the low volume of chips demanded by the government for space exploration and high-tech equipment, the factory was not being used at full capacity. The contractor decided to run some low-cost computer chips in the factory to fill the unused capacity. The chips were already designed and just needed to be manufactured. Soon, the contractor was producing the low-cost chips. Profit margins on the low-cost chips were low, but because the infrastructure and equipment were already in place, the contractor believed it would be easy to make a profit.

After six months of production, the contractor reviewed the profitability of the low-cost computer chips. The accounting data indicated that the contractor was actually losing money on every chip. When the reasons for the high cost were examined, the contractor found that the factory culture demanded extremely high quality. The facility typically manufactured high-tech computer chips designed for space exploration, and so employees stressed high quality because a failure in a computer chip in space could be catastrophic. Both the company culture and the manufacturing process had been created based on high expectations about quality. So, even though people knew the quality specifications for the low-cost chips were much lower than usual, the contractor's culture led them to apply the same processes and approaches.

After the cost analysis, the contractor decided not to continue manufacturing the low-cost chips. The only way to make a profit on the chip would be to change the culture that reinforced the quality and effectiveness of the contractor's core product.

Each company must understand how intended changes will impact company culture. A common mistake in implementing change is that people see how another company has implemented a change and naturally believe, if they approach the change in the same way, the results will be the same. But, more often, the existing company culture significantly impacts how changes are implemented.

> *A company was trying to improve quality. A root-cause analysis revealed that total quality initiatives were being impeded by the company culture, which centered on doing whatever customers wanted. Employees prided themselves on accomplishing the impossible for their customers. For example, if an employee specified a time of delivery, and the customer asked for delivery in half that time, the employee would still find a way to accomplish the task in half the time. Praise and recognition would be heaped on the employee by the customer. Occasionally, however, errors accompanied these Herculean efforts. The errors, though small, were viewed very negatively by customers.*
>
> *Company managers decided to set realistic time frames for delivery and then stand by them. Customer service representatives were instructed, "Just tell them 'no.' " But customers were not used to hearing "No." It didn't sound like the same company anymore. Other companies could stick to their deadlines, and for some reason it wasn't viewed by customers as negative. But the feedback from customers on the company's new policy was very negative. Also, employees didn't like to say, "No." It felt like they were not serving their customers as well. And even though employees had been given clear instructions on realistic time frames, the practice continued.*

The company's change process ultimately was very difficult. Customers had to be educated that error-free work was more important to them than a few weeks' turnaround. The company lost a few customers, but most customers began to plan their jobs better and the more realistic timing was built into their processes. Employees attended several training sessions that stressed the value of quality. Employees soon began to see that delivering a product in half the time but with errors was not serving the customer.

11. *Practicing*

We would never consider coaching an athletic team without scheduling time to practice. We wouldn't assume that people on the team would naturally know how to work together, or that every member of the team had the skills to execute plays well. New skills, new teams, and different approaches require practice. We should not expect performance to be high at first. New teams need good coaching, feedback, skill-building drills, and practice.

Sometimes practicing change is fairly straightforward; at other times, we may not know how to practice. Here are a few practice tips:

1. Have the team read an article or book.

2. Hold a training course on new skills required for the change.

3. Provide team members with instructional audio tapes.

4. Hold regular staff meetings and review the change process. Talk about successes, failures, and exceptional efforts. Role-play different situations.

5. Share your learning with other teams going through the same change.

6. Assign outside coaches or mentors to teams to help them work through difficult problems.

7. Organize field trips to visit other organizations that have mastered the skills or experiences your team needs.

8. Find ways to measure, implement, and keep track of progress.

9. Look for off-line opportunities to practice. Members of the team might get involved in community service or extra curricular activities to help them build required skills.

10. Look at systems and processes that support the change and those that distract from the change.

11. Recognize aspects of the company culture that make change difficult and brainstorm ways to integrate the change into the culture.

12. Be patient but persistent. Change takes time, but it also takes continued effort.

12. Avoiding Belief Traps

A building supply company made tubs and shower enclosures used primarily in new residential construction. In an effort to shore up their market share, the company conducted interviews with its 40 contractors. Prior to the interviews, the company also interviewed "internal customers," the employees who worked with contractors. As a group, the building contractors were characterized as unorganized and demanding. Stories circulated about how contractors would forget to order materials and then call up the same day materials were needed, demanding that something be installed.

On the other hand, interviews with building contractors seemed to highlight the complexity of their work. Contractors were expected to coordinate the efforts of several different subcontractors in a short period of time to produce a finished home on time with high quality. Some of the interviews with contractors were conducted over the phone, often either late at night or early in the morning when the contractors were in their home offices. The contractors seemed to be master jugglers who were very good at keeping dozens of projects going all at once.

After the interviews, the company constructed a profile to outline the average workday of a building contractor. It was frantic. When the profile was presented to employees, it was easy for them to see why contractors might frequently order late and be demanding. The employees were asked, "If you were a contractor, what kind of performance would you expect from your best subcontractors?" The employees answered that top subcontractors would need to be dependable, reliable, and responsive to short deadlines.

One employee suggested, "If I were a contractor, I would really value subcontractors that made my job and life easier. I have always thought the problem with most contractors was that they're not organized, and it must have been their own fault if they didn't get what they needed when they needed it. If a subcontractor came to me and said he or she would help me plan and order materials for each house, track progress, and oversee the installation, I would give that subcontractor all my business because it would make my life so much easier. If we did that for our contractors, our business would run much more efficiently, and we would get more business. The time it takes to plan for them would be less than the time it takes for us to react to their emergencies."

Until employees changed the way they thought about contractors, nothing would have changed in the customer relationship. But, by changing their thinking, many of the employees were able to build

*stronger relationships with contractors and improve
their business.*

In their book *Prisoners of Belief,* Matthew McKay and
Patrick Fanning indicate that core beliefs "define how you feel
about yourself and the emotional tone of your life."[3] Our
beliefs include our feelings about our competence and abilities,
attitudes about other people, stereotypes, values, and motives.

One of the employee beliefs was that contractors were
"unorganized and demanding." This belief was maintained
by a process called selective attention—only paying attention
to events that support our belief system and ignoring those
that don't. McKay and Fanning call this "mental grooving,"
falling into a rut that makes it easier to deal with people and
situations. We can break free from some of these self-defeat-
ing beliefs by first understanding our core beliefs and the
rules associated with those beliefs.

Principle 21: Changing behavior often requires changing core beliefs.

We can also go through the process of testing our beliefs in an
objective way. When we test our beliefs, we often recognize that
our rigid personal rules are not true. In the above case, as employees began to better understand the difficult work the contractors
had, it was no longer surprising that contractors might occasionally forget to order materials.

Finally, we can develop new beliefs that support and reinforce positive behavior. A psychological disorder called
"imagined ugliness" (body dimorphic disorder) shows how
this works. People with this disorder imagine they are ugly
when they are not. These people focus extensively on small
defects and exaggerate them: "My hands and fingers don't
look right." They focus all their attention on small, irrelevant
things. Therapy to help these individuals focuses on teaching
them to be more objective and realistic in their evaluations.

As you introduce a new change in an organization, ask yourself and others, "What beliefs, values, or rules do we have that *do not* support and reinforce what I am attempting to change?" Sometimes, to make a change in an organization, you must change common beliefs.

13. Shaping Goals and Behaviors

Sometimes organizations try to change things so complex or unique that the organization has little skill, experience, or expertise to complete the change. For example, an organization that had not used much technology in the past (e-mail, Internet, databases, or scheduling software) might try to change to incorporate the technology in all areas, but it may be difficult for the company to succeed with such a comprehensive change in the short-term. The company could hire an information systems professional to help, but that person can't make employees use the new systems. If organizations do not currently have the skills or expertise, they may find it difficult even to begin the change process. This is when shaping becomes helpful.

I first encountered "shaping" in an animal behavior class in college. I was assigned to train a rat to press a lever to get water. The animals had been deprived of water and then placed in the training cage with the lever. I waited patiently for the rat to press the lever, but it never even went close to the lever. By the end of the lab period, the rat was still thirsty, and it had made no attempt to press the lever. I felt very discouraged.

Then I learned about shaping. In shaping behavior, you reward successive approximations of a desired behavior. During the next lab period, I began by giving the rat a drink as soon as it turned toward the lever. Although turning toward the lever was not the final, desired result of pressing the lever, I couldn't train the rat to press the lever unless it got close to it. However, I could reward the rat for looking or moving in the right direction until it learned where the lever was.

Soon the rat began to turn quickly toward the lever. I would wait for the rat to turn and approach the lever before I rewarded it. I was amazed at how fast the shaping process worked. By the end of the second session the rat busily pressed the lever whenever it wanted water.

Principle 22: For some systems and processes, incremental change can create substantial change over time.

Organizational shaping is somewhat different from teaching tricks to rats, but the same principle applies. James Brian Quinn coined the phrase "logical incrementalism." Logical incrementalism means that organizations take small, incremental steps to achieve change.[4] Many organizations talk about frame-breaking change, but frame-breaking change is the opposite of logical incrementalism. Frame-breaking change means that everything totally changes overnight. Sometimes frame-breaking change does not work. It can destroy the culture and trust of an organization. But incrementalism, or organizational shaping, begins the change process with incremental steps.

In the technology example at the beginning of this section, the company might begin by getting everyone a computer. Then, after a few months it could install e-mail and a scheduling software program. After training the employees on how to use their computers, e-mail, and software, some of the employees may begin to use the new technology and incorporate it into their jobs. These employees can then become coaches and mentors to others. In one such example, a company went from being technologically backward to being a technology leader in a little over three years. By using an incremental approach to change, the company encountered little resistance to change. Also, the company saved money because the longer they waited, the lower the cost of the software and hardware became.

One warning about incrementalism: Many organizations use an incremental approach to change, but they never really change. The technique can be used to avoid making difficult decisions and to slow down when a fast move may be preferred. Incrementalism can make you feel like you're changing, but it can be mistaken for real change. In these cases, incrementalism is more like slow death than change.

14. Rewarding Change Efforts

As you try to implement changes, ask yourself if rewarding employee behavior or results will help implement a change. Too often, we embrace change for its own sake. Managers seem to believe that employees naturally want to change. Employees ask themselves, but never vocalize, things such as, "What is in this for me?" Keep in mind that rewards are not only money. Recognition, praise, competition, rewarding work, career opportunities, and new challenges often work as effectively as money. Some steps for linking rewards to change efforts include:

1. Determine desired outcomes. Be clear about desired outcomes. Set short-term, intermediate, and final outcomes before beginning change efforts. At first it may seem obvious, but many desired outcomes are difficult to quantify and measure. Such difficult-to-measure efforts may involve improving collaboration between groups, or increasing communication up and down the organization.

2. Find ways to measure or evaluate outcomes. Some things are easy to measure: profitability, waste, output, head count, costs, and so forth; other things are more difficult, such as intuitive or subjective judgments. For example, team effectiveness could be measured by having an objective committee evaluate each team.

3. Test the measurement system. Whenever there is a direct link between performance and rewards, make sure the measurement system is reliable. Look for ways people might manipulate the system to get desired rewards.

4. Brainstorm potential rewards. Don't assume money is the only way to motivate people. Brainstorm potential rewards and then match up rewards to different groups of people. Technical employees, for example, may be rewarded with new equipment while front-line employees may prefer time off.

5. Link outcomes and rewards. Once you determine the outcomes and rewards, decide next how to link them. Rewards can be linked in a fixed or variable fashion. Fixed rewards occur at specified intervals or at the occurrence of an outcome, such as sales commissions or profit sharing. Variable rewards occur more randomly, such as recognition of superb individual performance. With variable rewards, people may not get recognized every time they perform, but occasional recognition can be effective in reinforcing behavior. An example of a variable reward is occasionally buying lunch for a group of employees. At lunch, link the reward (lunch) to several outcomes that were achieved in recent months.

6. Communicate or demonstrate. Typically, fixed rewards require specific and detailed communication. People need to know "the rules of the game and how to play." Variable rewards can be demonstrated, such as recognizing people when you see the desired behavior, without being formally communicated.

7. Follow through. Research has shown that variable rewards tend to produce longer-lasting effects. But the problem with variable rewards is that it's easy to forget and allow the rewards to drop off. It's important to follow through until the change is well-established.

Caution: Rewards can be powerful. Keep the following rule in mind when establishing fixed rewards linked to pay:

"It's easy to give, but hard to take away." The following additional guidelines may help you establish a reward program without violating employee expectations:

1. Be clear about the reward period. Is the reward program for one year or forever?

2. Make sure your reward program is not set in concrete. Communicate up front with employees that you anticipate some modifications in the reward system. In a recent survey we evaluated a facility's gain-sharing program. One group was very negative about the program because it appeared to be impossible to achieve the gain-sharing reward. To make the plan fair, it needed to be calibrated.

3. Don't be too generous. Over-rewarding can teach you a tough lesson. Once when I was trying to get one of my children to read more, I offered one dollar for every book he read. I saw no change. I went to five dollars and still he didn't read, nor did he read when I raised the reward to seven dollars. At the ten dollar level he read 20 books in two months.

4. Look for negative side-effects of rewards. People learn quickly. If you reward them for outcome A and not for outcome B, then unless outcome B is a natural consequence of outcome A you will get less of outcome B.

5. Be Fair. Rewards can be morale killers for people that get left out. I find that nothing frustrates people more than when they work hard only to see others get the recognition.

15. Creating Structure to Support Change

I travel every week. In the past, I would go to the airport, park my car, and then run to catch my flight. A few days later when I returned I could never remember where I'd parked my car. I would eventually find the car, but it would sometimes take as much as 20 minutes of walking up and down the aisles to find it. This became very frustrating for me, especially at the end of long trips, and I had a great desire to change.

I remember trying several different techniques: I would try to make a mental picture of the area so I would remember it; or I would write down the row number on my parking ticket. These techniques seemed to work as long as I wasn't in a hurry, in which cases I was more worried about missing my plane than about remembering where I'd parked my car. Finally, I came across a structural solution to solve my problem. I found an area of the parking lot where I knew I could always find a place in approximately the same location every time. Now, although it's a little farther away, I can always remember where I'm parked. I don't have to worry about it anymore. And although my memory is not any better, I no longer have to remember. It always works.

Creating change in an organization is like walking a high-wire tight rope without a net. Creating structure to support change efforts is like adding a net, a balancing stick, and ropes on both sides to hang on to—just in case. Structure makes weak organizations strong and strong organizations stable. Like a large building, once structure is established, if you remove the structure the building collapses.

Principle 23: By framing proposed changes within a structured environment, most changes are easier to execute.

Structure includes systems, processes, procedures, and approaches that facilitate change. (*Figure 7 provides a list of structured and unstructured approaches to change efforts.*)

Information technology is now on the cutting edge for creating new systems and processes that can dramatically impact change efforts. For example, e-mail provides companies with the ability to communicate more quickly and at a lower cost than ever before.

Recently, one of my partners described a new client of ours from Greece. The client had purchased our product, but he had never physically met my partner or anyone at our company. I

Change Effort	Unstructured Approach	Structured Approach
Exercise at least three times per week.	Set a goal and write it down on paper.	Hire a trainer; buy exercise equipment; instruct trainer to come to your house and pull you out of bed if necessary.
Hold regular staff meetings.	Encourage groups to meet more often; set goals for how often the group should meet.	Schedule all group meetings for the year; have all group members include the schedule in their personal calendars.
Improve collaboration between groups.	Ask groups to collaborate and to give an occasional speech about the value of collaboration.	Set up monthly meetings between groups where collaborations must occur; ask them to share positive and negative feedback; reward groups who collaborate best.

Figure 7: Creating Structure to Support Change

asked how he had made the sale. He told me that, because of the time difference, they had only spoken on the phone once, but he had managed the sales process through e-mail. Having been an editor for the *Wall Street Journal,* he could quickly compose compelling and informative e-mail messages.

Likewise, an Intranet offers companies the ability to share information and provide a method of common access in the company. Sophisticated applications facilitate product ordering, customer service, billing, help systems, and analysis systems. This new information technology creates a tremendous advantage for those who learn how to take advantage of the technology. As you begin the change process, ask yourself how information technology could help you.

Many organizations are also experimenting with new organizational charts to facilitate change. Traditional company functions (R&D, Sales, Manufacturing, and so forth) are being replaced by new, cross-functional structures. These new structures can facilitate change. The new structures change the way people look at the world, the way people interact with others, and the way decisions are made. The new structures also change many traditional notions that employees have about careers, promotions, and development. (In traditional systems, functional specialists are promoted for functional expertise, but in the new systems, general skills are more highly valued although there is less opportunity for promotion.) Also, if you can align the organizational structure with the change process, you may find changes are easier to execute. Keep in mind, however, structural changes also impact many other systems and processes in the organization.

16. Building Organizational Confidence

Scott Adams, creator of "Dilbert," has been phenomenally popular lately. Part of the reason for his cartoon's popularity, is that Adams is very clever and creative. Many of his cartoons carry an underlying theme that I personally identify with, and I think others do, too. This underlying theme is that, in general, organizations don't care about people. This theme suggests that organizational programs, changes, and processes typically benefit the organization, and especially upper management, rather than the average employee. I think Scott Adams has done a great job of capturing the cynicism many feel toward organizations. I don't think Adams created Dilbert's cynicism, but he acts as a sort of therapeutic spokesman for the working class.

The cynicism that people hold toward companies is well-deserved by those companies. For the most part, organizations have fought for survival at the expense of many people. Organizations we once knew as career companies, where a person could work for an entire career, have either disappeared or destroyed the loyalty they once enjoyed.

Undertaking a change effort in an organization typically requires the commitment and involvement of employees. Often, employees are told how the new program will benefit them. Most employees probably greet this approach with some cynicism. It has become the exception rather than the rule that employees are not skeptical of change efforts. The following recommendations may help organizations deal with employee cynicism and foster employee confidence in company change efforts.

- *Anticipate cynicism.* Cynicism is inevitable.
- *Don't underestimate cynicism.* Employees have great expertise in passive resistance (saying the right things but doing nothing to help). Cynicism can kill a good change effort.
- *Be realistic.* What impact will change efforts really have on employees? Any program that improves organizational efficiency typically results in a smaller workforce. Employees know this will happen. Be clear about how and when reductions will occur.
- *Have good answers.* Tell people the truth; they can handle it, and you will be respected. If you're the messenger then push management to provide clear answers.
- *Involvement is key.* Employees tend to be less cynical about programs and changes they are involved in creating.
- *Walk in their shoes.* Will this change process pass your most cynical test? If not, don't do it. Employees aren't stupid. You may fool them once, but never twice.

17. *Involving Individuals in Organizational Change*

Often, managers who initiate organizational change don't fully recognize that for the change to be achieved, individuals must change their behavior. This is always implied but rarely explicit. Change efforts work best when individuals know what is expected. Individual expectations often are not clarified because they are not understood. When change efforts and goals remain at a global, general level, the individual changes required are never explicit. For example, if an organization is working to improve collaboration between groups, then the organization needs to define the individual behaviors to facilitate that collaboration. Making those behaviors explicit to employees and incorporating the employees into feedback and appraisal processes helps to reinforce the organizational change.

> *A fast-food restaurant chain conducted a cultural assessment and found three issues that needed immediate attention and change. The worldwide parent company established an action plan to create change in the overall organization. After evaluating the plan, directors asked, "If we successfully executed this action plan at the parent-company level, would that be enough to create the needed change?" The answer, of course, was "No."*
>
> *Everyone in the company felt that many aspects of the problem existed at all levels and locations of the organization. A plan was created to share the results of the cultural assessment throughout the organization in a planning session for company supervisors. Each person in the session would be asked to develop an individual action plan to address the three issues in their work group.*
>
> *At the work group level, the assessment results were then presented by the supervisor, and each individual was asked to create a development plan for one of the three issues on which they could take personal action. Driving the same three issues to every level of the organization, creating both the systems and the structural changes, along with individual behavioral changes made for a substantial difference in the company's performance in the three issues.*

Focusing on individual behavior impacts organizational change from two perspectives: One, if companies can get their organizational structure right, and align it with their strategy and systems, then people will adapt their behavior to those conditions; on the other hand, if companies can influence individuals to modify their behavior appropriately and then create systems and structures to support those behaviors, then the organization can change more quickly. In reality, both perspectives are true. Individuals find it easier to change when systems and processes are in place, but if they aren't in place, individuals may be lead or persuaded to fully utilize whatever systems and structures are in place.

18. Keeping the Effort Alive

One problem with change efforts is they are easier to start than to finish. Pushing change efforts to completion requires both persistence and patience. The following list of tips and hints may help you keep your change efforts going:

- *Be realistic* when you start that you will need to reinvigorate your efforts. When planning your change effort, consider how to keep it going by:
  - Checking progress.
  - Reporting on partial progress.
  - Creating events to motivate people.
  - Communicating frequently and consistently.
- *Don't get upset when things stall.* It's normal for change efforts to stall occasionally, but have a plan to restart your effort. Often, this shows employees that you are really serious about this change.
- *Generate short-term wins.* Break a big change effort down into smaller wins that can be celebrated and acknowledged.
- *Don't stop pushing too soon* or the organization will revert back. Employees learn to say the right things before the change is in cement. Some changes are like bad habits that come back if constant attention is not paid to the change.
- *Put systems, processes, and procedures in place* to support and reinforce the change effort.
- *Find natural opportunities to review progress* on changes, such as quarterly meetings or even annual events. Talk about your successes and remind employees about the additional effort required for success.

19. Empowering Employees

*An R&D lab for a large paper company had
empowered its employees at all levels with a clear
knowledge of the company's strategy and how it
could gain a competitive advantage by executing that
strategy well. Managers from another company came
to visit to observe the implementation of the strategy.
After it was briefed, the group was invited on a tour
of the facility. At the conclusion of the tour, the
group gathered in the lobby. A few visitors became
separated from the main group at the elevator, and,
as they were waiting for the next one, they conversed
with one of the employees who was also waiting.*

*They quizzed the employee about the company's
strategy and why changes were so critical to the
company's success. The visitors were quite impressed
with his answers and the enthusiasm he demonstrated. After rejoining the rest of the group, the
visitors who had been separated asked the host if he
knew the employee they had spoken with on their
trip down. "Yes," replied the host, "Robert is a
wonderful employee." The group asked what
Robert's job was in the facility. "Oh," replied the
host, "He's a janitor."*

*In a group meeting following the trip, group mem-
bers were asked what impressed them the most about
their visit. The consensus was "Robert, the Janitor."
The group of managers felt that if all employees
understood and were committed to the company's strategy, even down to the janitor, imagine the power an
organization would have to execute that strategy.*

With clear leadership, employees at all levels of the organization can be advocates for change. Some leaders find the

process of creating change to be a lonely process. They feel both isolated and unsupported. Most of the time, these leaders are also unsuccessful. For organizations to function effectively with leaner, flatter structures, employees at the bottom must be given additional influence and control. In the old command-and-control organizations, a few committed managers with a common shared vision could create change. But in today's lean, flat organizations, more people need to be committed to change efforts.

Employees at all levels not only need to be committed, but they also need to be knowledgeable. They need to see what the leaders see, understand what the leaders understand, and be as committed to the change as the leaders are. With employees at all levels focused on the same future, there can be tremendous power and great potential.

20. Making Tradeoffs

Most of the time, significant changes require some tradeoffs. The basic notion of tradeoffs is that, in order for a company to make a change, they must give up something. The following case illustrates this point:

> A small service organization felt it had been spending excessively and it was time to tighten the company's belts. All the key executives were present when the management group decided to take a hard look at the company's spending practices. Soon, a study was conducted, and recommendations were made that would result in major savings and improved profits. The executives met again to review the findings.
>
> As the first recommendations were reviewed, the executives as a group responded positively to the changes. The first recommendations focused on changes at lower levels of the organization. But the next set of recommendations focused on issues with

> *executives. Executives were not spending within their*
> *budgets, and some of the expenses were questionably*
> *of a personal nature. The executives all had person-*
> *al assistance, and one recommendation focused on*
> *cutting the amount of personal assistance in half.*
> *The executives became very defensive, claiming the*
> *spending level was a necessity. After some time, the*
> *executives began to see that to control spending, each*
> *would have to make some personal sacrifices.*

Once companies are clear about the changes they really want, they must also clarify the tradeoffs necessary to make those changes happen. You can rarely have it all, and, most of the time, to get one thing we really want, we must give up something else.

21. Focusing

Finally, organizations and individuals can pay attention only to a limited number of things at one time. Introducing too many initiatives, activities, or projects can divert the attention and effectiveness of an organization. Managers must act as gate keepers to limit the competing priorities allowable for the organization or group and each person in it. Most gate keepers, of course, try to eliminate "bad" initiatives or activities. But what they soon find is that very few initiatives or activities are "bad." Most seem to be good things to do, but there still are too many. The more activities allowed in your organization, the greater the distraction from the core activities that create competitive advantage.

The following list of tips can help you eliminate unwanted initiatives and activities.

• Is this activity linked directly to the core mission of your organization?

- If the organization were to focus its attention on this activity, is there evidence that the effectiveness or efficiency of accomplishing the core mission would improve?
- If you are required to do the activity because of a corporate mandate, and the activity is not directly linked to the company's core mission, find ways to minimize the distraction caused by the activity.
- Decide on a limited number of "charity" or "good corporate citizen" projects to be completed in one year. Once you select those projects, explain to those who continue to solicit your help that you officially sponsor only a tiny number of activities per year, and that you have already selected those activities.
- Annually review the activities and initiatives of your organization. Most organizations find up to 50 percent of their activities add no value to the company. Eliminate activities that add no value and focus on activities that add value.

In this chapter, 21 different recommendations were presented on how to create change in organizations. If anyone tries to do all 21, I predict their change efforts will be unsuccessful. We have found that, depending on the change your organization is going through and the culture of your organization, using a few of these suggestions at a time will help you to produce change.

Notes for Chapter 6

1. Gene Dalton, Louis B. Barnes and Abraham Zaleznik, *The Distribution of Authority in Formal Organizations,* Boston, MA: Division of Research, Harvard Business School, 1968, Chapter 5: "Change in Organizations" (Reprinted: Boston, MA: MIT Press, 1973).

2. Carole Hyatt and Linda Gottlieb. *When Smart People Fail: Rebuilding Yourself for Success.* New York: Penguin Books, 1987.

3. Matthew McKay and Patrick Fanning, *Prisoners of Belief: Exposing & Changing Beliefs That Control Your Life.* Oakland, CA: New Harbinger, 1991.

4. James Brian Quinn, *Strategies for Change: Logical Incrementalism.* Homewood, IL: Richard D. Irwin, 1980.

7

LEADING CHANGE

As organizations struggle to change, one critical ingredi-
ent remains unchallenged as a driving source for creating
meaningful change: leadership. Leadership is the ability to
get an organization excited, motivated, committed, to get it
to perform in new and better ways.

*Principle 24: Leadership is a critical skill
that can't be replaced in any successful
change effort.*

Leading change is partly genetic and partly learned and
developed. In this chapter I present ten characteristics of
effective leadership that differentiates effective leaders from
ineffective leaders. These characteristics are keys that, if
developed, can assist leaders in managing the change process.

The Executive Study

Recently, 275 executives received multi-rater assessment
surveys. The surveys contained 98 questions asking for written comments on the leader's strengths and weaknesses. The
survey measured 22 dimensions of executive behavior:

Vision, Monitoring the environment

Distinctive competence and communication of direction

Directive leadership

Managing commitments

Risk-taking

Meeting commitments

Organization

Incrementalism, Managing ambiguity

Personal competence

Building competence

Building trust

Confrontation

Exercising influence

Consideration

Integrity

Making tough decisions

Getting results

Persuasion

Representing

Networking

Availability

Sponsoring

Managing diversity

The executives distributed 12 surveys to their direct reports, peers, and bosses, and then completed one survey on themselves. When the surveys were completed, the 15 highest-scoring executives were compared to the 15 lowest-scoring executives using the 98-item survey as a measure of overall effectiveness. T-tests were computed to help understand which survey items best differentiated the highest- from the lowest-scoring individuals. Written comments were also reviewed for both groups to understand how high- and low-scoring executives were described. The items that best discriminated between high- and low-scoring executives were then factor-analyzed to create major clusters or factors.

The Problem with Conventional Wisdom

I recently read an article that advised executives on how to be more effective. The article recommended that executives arrive on time for meetings and appointments. Being late was described as critical mistake that would hurt a person's overall effectiveness. I found that interesting because in our study, we found an item that measured how often executives were late for appointments and meetings. We found that effective executives were no more likely to be rated highly for being on time than ineffective executives. This validated my own experience.

Some of the best leaders I know are often late for meetings, and some of the worst leaders I know are always on time. Other effective leaders are on time, and poor leaders always seem to be late, but the point is the tendency to be on time or late is not correlated with overall effectiveness. On the other hand, our study did, in fact, indicate which factors make the most difference. Of the 22 dimensions and 98 items researched, we determined that ten are key to leadership effectiveness.

Ten Differentiating Factors

The following ten factors were determined to be key differentiators between the best and worst leaders:

Getting Results

Integrity: Walking Your Talk

Trust and Respect

Vision and Confidence in the Future

Organization

Persuasion

Inspiration

Innovation and Experimentation

Analytical, Technical Competence

People Skills and Consideration

1. Getting Results

The best executives under "getting results" were described as:

- They play key roles in helping work units meet their deadlines.
- They are highly committed to meeting organizational goals and objectives.
- They have a can-do, never-say-die attitude.
- They make things happen rather than letting things happen.

A comment described one of the best executives in the following way, "He gives 100 percent of himself. He doesn't know everything, but he will help find a solution every time." The worst executives were seen as "letting things happen" or "accepting good enough as good enough." The worst executives were told they needed to "step up and take charge," and that too often they were "satisfied with slip-shod work."

The best executives in our study knew the difference between driving for activity and driving for results. Driving for activity is keeping people busy, while driving for results keeps people focused on delivering key results: a huge and important distinction. People who scored high on driving for results were not afraid to push for higher levels of effort and production than people who generally felt comfortable. The key to keeping employees performing at high levels is to get employees to push themselves for higher effort rather than having managers push them.

2. Integrity: Walking Your Talk

Those who "walked their talk" were perceived more positively than those who couldn't be trusted or who had questionable integrity. Executives with high integrity were described as:

- They are trusted to *not* take advantage of people or the organization.
- They *do not* use coercive or position power to get what they want.
- They *never* cause others to question the executives' integrity because of actions.
- They are honest in their dealings with others.
- They practice what they preach.
- They *never* say one thing and do another.

Written comments described the best executives as: "Stands up for his employees, always, even when we're wrong. He'll take the blame, and he never blames us when things go wrong." "He has the highest integrity and commitment of any manager in the company." "His integrity is unquestionable. I have never seen it waiver."

The worst executives were described in the opposite way: "When things go wrong, she fingers the blame on subordinates." "Does not practice what he preaches. He parrots his boss, but doesn't believe in it." "He's too political to have integrity." "I question her integrity because of her overriding sense that her primary objective is to promote herself." "He is wishy-washy, bouncing back and forth between differing arguments."

Integrity is a key behavior of effective leaders. We are quick to judge our leaders' integrity. Integrity is difficult to maintain all the time. Any slight indiscretion can often be perceived as a total loss. Working issues to make them politically correct is also typically seen as a loss of integrity. Integrity is easy to lose and difficult to regain in the perceptions of others.

3. Trust and Respect

Executives are judged as trusted and respected based on hundreds, or even thousands, of actions and interactions over time. Integrity helps build trust, and good business competence and technical skills help build others' confidence in executive judgment. The best executives under "trust and respect" were described by others as:

- Others have confidence in their business judgment.
- They are respected and trusted by those with whom they work.
- They build up credit and trust with others in the organization.

Written comments described the best executives as: "Fair, understanding, and trusted." "Trusted totally." "He's the most trustworthy person in the company." "Very high level of trust; can keep confidences." "Never has given a reason to inspire anything but absolute trust."

The worst executives were described with the following comments: "He is insincere. There's usually a gap between his real and declared aims, necessitating the use of long words and exhaustive idioms. There is always a hidden agenda in dealing with him." "He isn't to be trusted. He tries to hide things and then springs them on people. Often, he contradicts previous communications." "Not much trust. People know it doesn't take much from management to have him change his position." "Trust can't be commanded. It needs to be earned from each individual." "There is a sense of mistrust for him throughout the community." "He is primarily concerned with promoting himself."

4. Vision and Confidence in the Future

There's a difference between doing work and working to achieve a vision. "Doing work" is activity, while "working to achieve a vision" is results. The key to delivering results versus activity is vision. The best executives have a clear vision and can share that vision with others. The worst executives have goals, objectives, and work, but they have little vision. The best executives were described as follows:

- They provide a definite sense of direction and purpose.
- They have a clear vision of the future of this organization.
- They make others feel this company is going someplace.

Written comments described high performers as: "Continually provides updated clarification." "Has frequent staff meetings to keep us all focused in one direction." "Is always the optimist, tries to stay one step ahead by looking at long-range plans." "He not only articulates well the end objectives of the organization, but also the methods and mechanisms needed to achieve them."

Written comments on the worst executives indicated: "Needs to work on strategic planning: Where are we going?" "There is a great amount of frustration caused by his ever-changing clear vision." "Direction is provided from the bottom up ('You guys know where we need to go')." "Seems satisfied to let others decide the role of his organization." "Tries to communicate a vision, but he comes across as insincere and aloof."

Those who lack vision do so because they lack clear understanding of products and the needs and concerns of customers. They lack the breadth of understanding needed to provide a broad perspective. They may have in-depth views about one aspect of the business, but that doesn't make the person a visionary. They lack energy and initiative to engage others in conversations that lead to in-depth visions rather than rehearsed paragraphs created by upper management.

5. Organization

The best executives are jugglers. They keep 50 balls in the air at once and rarely drop one. The ability to organize activities quickly, use brevity, and manage time is a key skill of the best executives. The best executives were described as:

- They are organized and know what to do next.
- They don't waste time on matters of low importance or value.
- They anticipate problems and work on them before they become a crisis.
- They spend enough time with those they work with.

Written comments of the best executives described them as: "He is always on top of things, both efficient and punctual, never flustered." "Has a good vision in identifying priorities." "Excellent time management skills." "Organized, efficient, and punctual." "Seems to utilize his direct reports and administrative staff well. Items do not back up on his desk."

The worst performers were described differently: "His nickname is 'Captain Chaos.' " "Loosely organized." "Creates the impression of going in many different directions at once." "Unorganized and inefficient. Often assigns single projects to multiple people only to end up with overlapping efforts."

6. Persuasion

The best executives have the ability to persuade others to accept their position. It takes skill to generate a clear vision, but the key to effectiveness is persuading others that your vision is correct. Delivering results is a key attribute, but the ability to persuade others to deliver excellent results is a critical part for effective executives. High-performing executives were described as:

- They are able to clearly articulate their positions.
- They are able to persuade others to accept their positions.
- They have a personal style that helps win others over to their positions.
- They are able to represent the organization to critical groups outside the organization.
- They present an appropriate company image both inside and outside the organization.
- They champion projects so others understand and support them.

Written comments on the best group of executives expressed a very positive view of their abilities to persuade others: "Able to convey the most complex issues in simple terms." "Easily persuades those who are easily swayed, and sometimes persuades even the most opinionated." "Wins people over many times with sheer enthusiasm." "He persuades with hardcore data, facts, figures, and past experience, not with 'hunches' or 'gut feelings.' "

Written comments for the worst executives showed low ability to persuade others: "Is not effective at persuasion. Lacks diplomacy, tends to be confrontational and emotional." "Very strong and emotional at times. Tends to dictate." "Likable, but not persuasive." "He gets his way by ordering, but I don't think he can persuade a worker or a peer." "Rarely clearly articulates his position."

7. *Inspiration*

The best executives lift others above what is normal or ordinary, get people to do more than they thought possible, build people up, and get people excited. The best executives are inspirational, not merely transactional. The best executives were described as:

- They energize people to go the extra mile.
- They inspire people to care about and strive for excellent performance.

Written comments described the best performers as: "Leads through his own example." "He inspires confidence." "There is no one I know that doesn't have confidence in him."

The worst performers were described very differently. It was evident from written comments that people could be very clear about what inspiration is not: "He seems to have plateaued or 'burned-out' in his job. He seems tired of management problems, challenges, and changes." "I believe he is competent, but he comes across as a 'bean-counter' and 'nitpicker'; he doesn't inspire or motivate those who work with him." "He operates on the 'I'm the boss' principle, which doesn't work." "When backed up by resistance, he often relies on 'that's the way the big guy wants it.'" "He relies on his physical properties—his voice and size." "Makes people feel unimportant."

8. *Innovation and Experimentation*

Most executives face many challenges. Simply "working harder" will not solve those challenges. There simply isn't enough time in the day or night to hit the aggressive targets that most executives are given. The best executives work smarter, not just harder. The smart part of their job involves finding ways to do work differently. Innovation is the key to future success. Successful executives who think outside the box and pursue new and different ideas are described as:

• They constructively challenge others to question the usual way of looking at things.

Written comments for the best describe innovative executives as: "Imaginative solutions." "Always pushing and encouraging others to find ways to do things better." "Refuses to accept 'it's always been done this way' as an adequate reason to do something." "Willing to bend the rules."

The worst performers were described very differently: "Has an aversion to trying new ideas unless he can be certain of the outcome; this causes frustration among subordinates." "Rarely looks at ideas unless they are shoved down his throat!" "Comes from the 'don't rock the boat' school of thought."

9. Analytical, Technical Competence

The ability of executives to understand technical issues is critical in the success of many organizations. We admire executives who can provide a simple yet comprehensive vision of the future. That simple vision is constructed after a thorough analysis of facts, figures, and projections. The best executives have the ability both to comprehend technical and financial data quickly and to formulate insightful conclusions that lead the organization forward. The best executives are described as:

• They are able to make effective business decisions based on an excellent understanding of financial, economic, market, and organizational data.

• They make decisions that reflect an understanding of the needs of the total business rather than the needs of small parts of the organization.

• They do not seek quick-fix solutions to complex problems when more understanding and study are needed.

Written comments describe these executives as: "Very competent; has the respect of his work unit as well as the organization." "Quick comprehension and assimilation of complex situations." "There is no questioning his competence. He possesses one of the brightest analytical minds in his profession." "Has demonstrated his ability to deal with the most complicated issues."

The worst executives were described in a very negative light: "Sometimes goes off half-cocked." "Persons in this work unit, right down to the clerks, have absolutely no confidence in his abilities or competence."

10. People Skills and Consideration

The final skill in which the best executives show substantially more ability than the worst executives is "people skills and consideration." Even though it is listed last, it is not the least important. The ability to understand the needs and concerns of others, to listen, and to act considerately are huge assets for any executive. Many people think they have these skills, but the only way to know is to be evaluated by others. Some people see this competency as opposite of the drive for results, but it's only through the use of people skills that the best executives can get employees to deliver excellent results. The best performers are described as:

- Even in disagreements, they listen to and respect the ideas of others.
- They are considerate of how their decisions or policies will affect others.
- They are considerate of others' interests when making decisions or formulating policies.

Written comments described the best executives as: "Works with you as opposed to you working for him." "I have never witnessed him ever putting anyone down, even when it's their fault. He will help where needed and even work side by side if that is needed."

The worst executives were not viewed positively in terms of people skills: "It is very difficult to discuss problems with him. His favorite line is, 'That's your problem.' " "Even though he compliments employees, it doesn't sound sincere. Was this rehearsed or learned in a management seminar?" "Too many 'cookbook' management techniques." "People don't feel comfortable in his presence."

Leading Change

The ten factors of the most competent executives provide an excellent model for evaluating individual effectiveness. As you read through the descriptions of the best and worst executives, rate yourself on each dimension. You may find some dimensions were not as positive as others. Keep in mind that people typically rate themselves more positively than others do.

If, in your self-evaluation, you feel there are some areas where you need improvement, you may still be a highly effective leader. In our research we found that the best leaders were not perfect in all ten dimensions, but they were very strong in at least seven. Some executives have one extraordinary strength and then back up that strength with very good skills in several other areas. As executives raise their effectiveness in several areas, they also get some halo effect as others begin to rate them higher than they actually are because the executive is so positive in an important dimension. We have also found that people can develop effectiveness in all ten dimensions. The development process requires:

- *Accurate assessment of current strengths and weaknesses.* These skills are only developed when people are clear about where they currently stand. Helping leaders understand their strengths and providing accurate, candid, and regular feedback on where they need to improve is key to increasing effectiveness.
- *Good coaching and mentoring.* Good athletes have good coaches. Good leaders also have good coaches. It's critical in many of these skills that people receive good coaching and mentoring.
- *Study and training opportunities.* Good training programs can help people practice critical skills and understand both the theory and application of each skill of leadership effectiveness. Good leaders are well-studied.

- *Challenging assignments that provide effective learning environments.* Executives may develop these critical skills when they are given assignments in learning environments where it is possible to make mistakes without the loss of position or status. Do-or-die assignments do not provide learning when the unsuccessful individual will be fired.
- *A "safety net" for people who shouldn't be executives.* Many technical professionals take on leadership assignments, only to find they are not as effective as they had hoped to be. Often, they don't even enjoy the work. Organizations can provide meaningful and challenging options for these individuals who can provide technical leadership better than the leadership of people.

8

CONCLUSION

There are no overnight transformations. Both organizational and individual change does not occur automatically. When employees provide feedback, however, they expect immediate change. My experience is that change occurs only through sustained effort over time. Most people are not optimistic about the extent to which change occurs in others. When asked how often they see significant changes in others, most people say, "Rarely." Change is often hard to see. But, when we ask people how often they see long-term growth in others, they say, "Frequently."

When I go on a trip for a week and come home, my children always look different. They have changed, and I can see it. I don't notice the changes when I'm with them all week. That's because the changes are really slow growth.

We tend to accept and be satisfied with our current circumstances. Otherwise, we would feel we are failing in our attempts to change, leading to the perception that we are failing as individuals. Processing feedback can be difficult. When we receive feedback, we often perceive that we are failing. We assume our failures are well-disguised and that they are not common knowledge, but almost everyone who knows us well is acquainted with our failures and the failures of the groups and projects we manage. Our successes, however, are not as easily recognized.

I do not recommend foolhardy experimentation in attempting change. I recommend consistent, calculated efforts to improve. None of us has "arrived." New and different challenges face us every day. Even the process of aging creates situations that make change necessary to maintain our effectiveness. The risks of change are always highest when you attempt to change alone. Involving others in your change efforts not only improves the odds of change, but also provides motivation for improvement.

You have the capacity to receive feedback, accept feedback, and make positive change. No person can force you to change, and no one can change for you. To change, you have to try. If you try, you might fail, but you can learn from your failures and produce the desired result—making feedback work.

Principles

PRINCIPLE 1: Asking others for input increases their expectation that you will change in a positive way. *(Page 11)*

PRINCIPLE 2: If you receive feedback but do not change for the better, you will be perceived more negatively than if you had not received feedback. *(Page 11)*

PRINCIPLE 3: You cannot change what you do not believe needs to be changed. *(Page 13)*

PRINCIPLE 4: It is better to receive negative feedback than to receive no feedback at all. *(Page 13)*

PRINCIPLE 5: Rather than accept insults and abuse, we tend to denounce not only what is said but those who say it. *(Page 14)*

PRINCIPLE 6: You can safely assume that all perceptions are real, at least to those who own them. *(Page 15)*

PRINCIPLE 7: You need to balance the interpretation of survey feedback to deal effectively with it. *(Page 17)*

PRINCIPLE 8: People must have a "felt need" to change, or they will not change. *(Page 22)*

PRINCIPLE 9: Others see things differently than we see them. *(Page 27)*

PRINCIPLE 10: To change the impressions others have, we must first understand how they see and experience things. *(Page 28)*

PRINCIPLE 11: When we provide feedback, we tend to base our perceptions on our own performance and personality. *(Page 33)*

PRINCIPLE 12: The better you understand the attribution process, the more you can make it work to your advantage. *(Page 36)*

PRINCIPLE 13: The first key to making a change is to increase your motivation and commitment to making the change. *(Page 43)*

PRINCIPLE 14: Involving others in change efforts increases the probability that change will occur. *(Page 49)*

PRINCIPLE 15: The most critical skill in making a change based on feedback is deciding what specific issue to work on first. *(Page 53)*

PRINCIPLE 16: Issues dealing with things are much easier to change than those dealing with people. *(Page 58)*

PRINCIPLE 17: An organization's history and experience help determine which skills and processes will be most useful in a successful change effort. *(Page 69)*

PRINCIPLE 18: Organizations cannot stop to implement changes; they must change while they continue to execute. *(Page 72)*

PRINCIPLE 19: Before announcing any change, managers should build a broad support base for the change, including input from stakeholders at various organizational levels. *(Page 74)*

PRINCIPLE 20: Redefining negative feedback in a positive light creates increased motivation to change. *(Page 84)*

PRINCIPLE 21: Changing behavior often requires changing core beliefs. *(Page 90)*

PRINCIPLE 22: For some systems and processes, incremental change can create substantial change over time. *(Page 92)*

PRINCIPLE 23: By framing proposed changes within a structured environment, most changes are easier to execute. *(Page 97)*

PRINCIPLE 24: Leadership is a critical skill that can't be replaced in any successful change effort. *(Page 107)*

About Joe Folkman

Joe Folkman is a founding principal of Novations Group, Inc., where he helps organizations design assessment tools and feedback processes for organizational and individual improvement. He has over twenty years of experience in survey research, analysis, and consulting in organizational diagnosis, management assessment, customer service analysis, and managing both large-scale and individual change processes. He has developed measurement tools to assess an organization's strategic alignment and its readiness for change.

Folkman is the author of *Turning Feedback into Change,* and he has received a masters degree in organizational behavior and a doctorate in social and organizational psychology from Brigham Young University. He has conducted extensive research in psychometrics, survey research, statistical analysis of survey data, and organizational and individual change. His research has been published in the *Wall Street Journal, Personnel,* and *Executive Excellence,* among other publications, and he has designed and written numerous software programs to help companies gather and analyze feedback survey data.

For over fifteen years, Joe has consulted with a variety of top companies around the world, including Amoco, Boeing, Canadian Imperial Bank of Commerce, Cisco Systems, Eaton, Exxon, General Mills, Hewlett-Packard, McGraw-Hill, Mobil, Nortel, Novell, Phillips Petroleum, Rockwell, and Weyerhauser.

He lives in Orem, Utah, with his wife, Laura, and their five children: Brandon, Rachel, BreAnne, Matthew, and Corbin.

ABOUT NOVATIONS GROUP, INC.

Novations Group, Inc., is a founding member of PROVANT, Inc., an international consulting and training organization consisting of seven affiliated firms with expertise in such areas as communication, diversity, multimedia learning, retail sales training, human resource management, and behavioral sciences. Novations is a rapidly growing strategy and human resource management consulting firm with offices in New York, Texas, and Utah. Its mission is to develop individual capability while achieving business results. For over 20 years it has been serving some of the best companies in North America and Europe in areas of strategy clarification, organizational design, and competency. As one of the largest corporate survey firms in the nation, Novations is perhaps best known for its 360-degree surveys and organizational assessments. The company has emerged as an industry leader in providing a broad range of helpful survey and profile instruments for individuals and companies including:

Organization Assessments
Organizational Analysis Survey
Strategic Alignment Survey
Total Quality Survey
Customer Service Survey

Management and Leadership Development
Managing Individual and Team Effectiveness
360° Competency Profiles
Customized Leadership Profiles

Team Assessments
Team Development Survey
Team Effectiveness Profile

Novations' surveys and profiles consist of both written and numerical response data. In addition to unlimited demographic comparisons, the company's extensive database allows for surveys to be compared with national, company, group, and industry norms where available. Support services include customization of standardized instruments, survey administration, Internet and on-line data processing, data interpretation, presentation of results and recommendations, and development of activities such as strategic alignment and long-term planning.

To obtain customized feedback surveys for organizational assessment, individual profiles and analysis, or to receive information on Novations' workshops and conferences, please contact:

Novations Group, Inc.
5314 North 250 West, Suite 320
Provo, UT 84604
phone: (801) 375-7525
fax: (801) 375-7595
www.novations.com